HEALING YOUR HEART

Rewrite Your Story
with Awareness and Intention

Tris Thorp

PUBLISHING

Healing Your Heart: Rewrite Your Story with Awareness and Intention
By Tris Thorp

Copyright © 2018 by Tris Thorp

Crescendo Publishing, LLC
2-558 Upper Gage Ave., Ste. 246
Hamilton, ON L8V 4J6
Canada

GetPublished@CrescendoPublishing.com
1-877-575-8814

ISBN: 978-1-944177-96-6 (p)
ISBN: 978-1-944177-97-3 (e)

Printed in the United States of America
Cover design by Belinda Pearl / ArtandWord.com

10 9 8 7 6 5 4 3 2 1

Message from the Author

Click on the link below the image to hear
a special message from Tris.

https://www.youtube.com/
watch?v=8kxWEfQwVzU&feature=youtu.be

FREE GIFT for YOU!

Guided Meditation on Loving Kindness and Compassion

The path of life is beautiful. It's full of love, it's laden with opportunities and filled with kind, loving, and compassionate people.

And life can also be difficult, full of challenges, growth, and circumstances that can leave us feeling confused, disappointed and directionless.

The best chance we have at overcoming the more difficult times is to search for the gifts in our struggles, lean into love and learn how to be happy from the inside out.

I'd like to share my FREE GIFT with you –

A complimentary guided meditation on

Loving Kindness and Compassion.

Download your gift here:

tristhorp.com/healing-your-heart/

Endorsements

"Healing Your Heart is a must read if you are ready and willing to do the work required to gain an intimate look at how emotions shape your personal experience so you can heal your past and live your best life."

- Deepak Chopra

"Healing Your Heart can help you finally let go of your emotional baggage to become your true self and experience the life you were meant to live. Weaving together multiple wisdom traditions and personal experience, Tris Thorp has a deep understanding of the tools you need to move beyond unresolved wounds and emotions. Through awareness and self-compassion, she guides you through a process to unravel your past so you can unlock your future. If you are feeling stuck in your emotions and are ready to change, this book is for you!"

- Valencia Porter, MD, MPH,
Author of *Resilient Health:
How to Thrive in Our Toxic World*

"The heart is the mediator (or balancer) between the mind and the voice of Higher Self. In life, you need to include your heart in all actions and that is impossible to do when there is unresolved emotional baggage clouding your senses.

In her book, Healing Your Heart, Tris shares a profound and inspirational approach to connect with and heal your heart. There is nothing more powerful than living your life in a clear and heart-centered way, and Tris is the perfect guide for showing you how to do this."

- Dr. Matt James

"Once in a great while, an author comes along who speaks to me. Tris Thorp speaks to each and every one of us who has ever struggled to make sense out of life and its permutations. Beautifully written, yet pragmatic. Philosophical and deeply spiritually moving and with speith specific guidelines and practices for healing. A must read!"

- Dr. Patrick Scott
Clinical Assistant Professor of Psychiatry,
University of Nevada, Las Vegas School of Medicine

"Healing Your Heart is a practical, effective guide to reclaiming your life and healing the past. Through a series of simple, yet powerful techniques, Tris not only guides you in identifying what is holding you back, but she also provides concrete tools and exercises that will enable you to release that which no longer serves you. As a teacher and coach, Tris has a delightful balance of showing tremendous compassion, yet at the same time, being firm and direct. Healing Your Heart is one of those books you re-read every couple of years to get a soul tune-up. This is on my "required reading" list for anyone in search of transformation."

- Michelle Kole, Ph.D.,
Licensed Clinical Psychologist

Table of Contents

Foreword 5

1. Why Do This Work? 9
The Good, Bad, and Ugly of Emotions 11
The Baggage We Carry 12
Letting Your Baggage Go 15
Journaling 16

2. Preparation for the Journey 23
Compassionate Self-Inquiry 24
Key Principles for Transformation 28
Our Commitments 34
Are You Ready and Willing? 39

3. A Primer on Your Internal World: Your Emotions 43
Emotions 44
The 90-Second Rule 45
Our Emotions are Derived from our Needs 47
How Emotions Become Toxic 48
Inception of Illness 50
Secondary Gain 56

4. Your Internal World: The Unconscious 59
How Your Unconscious Mind Works 59
It's All in Your Perception 61
Emotional Toxicity: Limiting Beliefs 62
Emotional Toxicity: Unconscious Decisions 68
Components of Story Creation 71

5. Inventory Your World 77
How to Lay the Foundation 77
Easing into the Process 81
Questions for Digging up Baggage 85

What If You Can't Identify an Event?..93
Leaning into It...95
Beware of Distractions 97

6. Releasing What No Longer Serves You 99

Technique #1: Personification 100
Technique #2: Become the Observer to Reduce Your
Emotional Charge 105
Technique #3: Releasing Anxiety..107
Technique #4: Forgiveness 111
Why Forgive? 112
Getting to the Heart of the Matter 113
Forgiveness Process..117
Self-Forgiveness 120
The Key is Surrender..126
Ongoing Process.. 127

7. Navigating the Now..129

Trading Old Strategies for New...131
Changing Your Interpretation 136
Taking Responsibility...142
Break Old Patterns, Create Positive Habits..........................142
Dealing with Difficult Emotions in the Now 146
Using the Five Questions for Navigating the Now.................148
Own and Release the Emotion 152
Handling Emotions in the Midst of "Battle" 153

8. Your Emotional Support System...............................157

Mindfulness 160
Recapitulation 162
Reframing...164
Meeting Our Needs from Within 166
Strengthening Your Emotional Body 174
Practicing Emotional Intelligence.. 177

9. Conscious Communication.................................185
    Four Questions for Conscious Communication........................186
    Conscious Versus Unconscious Communication 190
    The Importance of Boundaries.......................................195

This is Not the End, It's Just the Beginning...............205
About the Author...207
Connect with the Author 209
Acknowledgements.......................................211
References......................................213
Resources..215

My Sincerest Thanks...

In this book, we will spend a lot of time healing ourselves from the people and experiences in our past that prevented us from being our best, from doing what we were meant to do, and from having the things we deserved to have.

Through the processes I share with you, you will discover that the people who have assisted in bringing you to your lowest points in life deserve as much gratitude as the people who have assisted you in getting to your highest points. Those who have caused us the most pain are the ones who have shown us our greatest strengths.

While it would be easy for me to thank all the people who have helped me along my path and supported me in achieving my goals and dreams, because of the material in and nature of this book, I've chosen to thank people who played key roles in enabling me to reach my lowest points.

To anyone who has ever violated a boundary, burned a bridge, or assisted me in hitting a low point in my life, I thank you. Your presence in my life enabled me to learn who I am, how to set boundaries, and become the empowered woman I am today.

Although we may never cross paths again, I am forever grateful for all you taught me.

Tris Thorp

Dedication

This book is dedicated to the late Dr. David Simon—my teacher, my mentor, and my friend. You helped me to see my dharma and set me on the path of healing my heart. In turn, I now get to help others find their own emotional healing. I wish you were here to see how beautifully things have turned out, and I know you are always with me in spirit.

"The greatest contribution we can make to the wellbeing of those in our lives is to have peace in our own hearts. When our hearts are filled with gratitude and our minds are brimming with enthusiasm, everyone we encounter leaves our space feeling a little bit lighter than when they entered it."

- David Simon,
Co-Founder and Medical Director – Chopra Center

Foreword

You were born whole, perfect, and pure. In fact, in the flickering moments as you took your very first steps out of the womb, you were unconditioned—your entire life story unwritten... yet pregnant with possibilities. Science now confirms that the Universe was birthed at the heart of a star. And, as you came into this world, you too began an expansive stardust journey of magnificent individuation.

The stage was set. The comforting nine-month soundtrack of your mother's beating heart was replaced by your own unique rhythm. And, without a playbook, much experience, or any tools to ensure your success, you began to weave a fabric of how you would interact with the world—thought by thought, thread by thread, need by need, and desire by desire. And, in your earliest days, you tried your best to please those around you so they would feed you, bathe you, change your diaper, hold you, and love you.

In time, your core needs of attention, affection, appreciation, and acceptance became more overt, and your deeper needs of the heart began to awaken in more intricate ways. Your basic methods of communicating also gave way to more articulate expressions as you recognized who and what would bring you comfort in a given moment.

Over the years, you began making interpretations and guesses about how situations should unfold and what others thought, believed, and did. You developed patterns of conditioned behavior, and soon your physiological and biological prerequisites evolved into more complex emotional requests. As you continued to navigate life's twists and turns, you crafted a distinct identity, like a character in a book or a role in a play. And—as you moved through the various phases of your life—you expanded, contracted, and refined that persona according

5

to those needs of the moment. You wrote and rewrote your story, ultimately reinforcing the previous chapter with each new page.

Each of us makes choices based on what we think we need to do in order to receive the love and feel the sense of belonging we all so desperately crave. But what we often don't realize is that these critical life decisions are mostly experimental, because life unfolds in unexpected ways—and *in real time*— and we haven't necessarily practiced our best responses to unknown situations.

That means that we are writing the narrative as it's occurring. We stumble at times, often leaving little room for our best version to shine forth. In some cases, we thrive and soar. And, in others, it's a dumbing down of our best expression. As we learn a little bit more about how life "works," we justify certain choices by telling ourselves little white lies like "It will get better after this," or "I only need to pretend in this moment." Out of fear or desperation, we sometimes make decisions that box us into corners we never expected to find ourselves in.

All the time, we are writing our story and reinforcing it through outcomes that confirm we have either made the right choice, or—through rationalizing and self-fulfilling prophecies— that we have made the wrong choice. We can beat ourselves up pretty harshly in those darker outcomes. And, in those uncertain moments, so far from our original plan, we defer our dreams and resign ourselves to accepting smaller expressions of our magnificence until our once-bright light begins to dim.

As the years go on, we forget that divine stardust moment of our birth and get further and further away from our innate knowledge of our wholeness, perfection, and purity. With each mistake or regretful action, we stop *accepting* that we are divine creations. We begin to build walls in our heart, our conversations, our sense of self, our attitudes, and even in our physical body. Our fear of being judged makes us seek to fit in, please others instead of ourselves, and our natural state of self-acceptance and self-celebration starts to fade. We become masters of hiding our vulnerability behind masks of stoicism and projections of false confidence. And, in the process, we lose the precious gift of innocence and become skeptical of the infinite kindness of the Universe. This is how the divinity in our soul is tamed. We all respond differently to this process, but everyone goes through these moments, and everyone makes compromises—big and small. The narrative continues... this is the story of everyone.

We realize that we've faltered along the way, we can't step back in time... we can't un-ring the bell. But we can make new, life-affirming, conscious choices that will allow us to heal, get back on track, and ultimately thrive. If we are mindful and honest with ourselves, we can introduce a pattern interrupt into the story, break the cycle, and begin a new, fresh, bold trajectory. We can re-set our course, re-establish ourselves in the present moment, vision new dreams, and begin writing a brand-new chapter of our life.

New beginnings are possible if we give ourselves permission to gently, lovingly, openly, and tenderly peel away the layers of our past that no longer serve us to reveal that sweet, pure perfection that is at the center of our being. If we can allow the veils of limiting beliefs to fall away and the pain of our emotional wounds to begin the process of healing, then we can return to the fractal of our wholeness, launch a fresh trajectory of emotional freedom, and reclaim true happiness in our life—which is our birthright. In this state of rebirth, you *can* flip the script and weave the fabric of a healed, whole, beautiful, brand-new existence.

There are many passageways to this brave new world. And I celebrate the fact that you have chosen Tris Thorp as your guide on this mindful path to living intentionally and making new, purposeful decisions to move your life from where you are to where you'd like to be.

In the pages that follow, Tris—a brilliantly adept life-student, a master of the ancient teachings of Vedanta, and a visionary teacher of heart-healing—provides the comprehensive blueprint for transcending the blockages and constrictions of your past and stepping into your best version. For more than a decade, she has immersed herself in a powerful fusion of ancient, time-tested practices with modern, cutting-edge scientific techniques, leading to transformational results in her own life and those of her students.

She has learned the evolutionary best-practices and subtle nuances for shattering limiting beliefs, making peace with the past, setting courageous boundaries, and rewriting your old story. With each step that you take with Tris on your journey back to wholeness, you will experience healing in all aspects of your life. So, right now, whatever route you have taken to arrive here, you hold at your fingertips the power to turn it all around—the power of rebirth, renewal, and reinvention.

As you navigate through life with *Healing Your Heart* as your true north of emotional healing, I am confident that every aspect of your life will unfold with greater ease, expanded happiness, and deeper fulfillment. Enjoy the journey. The best is yet to come!

~ davidji, Author of *Secrets of Meditation*

1

Why Do This Work?

*"Your task is not to seek for love but merely
to seek and find all the barriers within
yourself that you have built against it."*
- Rumi

If you're reading this book, I'm guessing that you're feeling stuck somewhere in your life. You're struggling with fear around not knowing who you really are, where your relationship is going, or whether your career is the right one. You might have a vague sense that things could be better, but you can't figure out what that looks like or how to get there. You probably don't know what you're doing—or not doing—to end up in the exact same painful relationship, dead-end job, shallow friendships, or unhealthy habits you've found yourself in time and time again. You might even be wondering if this is just normal. That only special people get to live fulfilling lives, and you're not one of them.

I get how feeling stuck or lost and fumbling through life with no real purpose or direction is deeply frustrating. I empathize with how you may be spinning out because life is happening too fast and you just can't seem to find a harmony between work, family, relationship, health, and fun. I can say these things, because it wasn't that long ago that I was going through the exact same thing.

I was operating on auto-pilot (in what is known as the Iago trance) and just going through the motions day after day, taking whatever life decided to throw my way. I felt frustrated, anxious, lost, disappointed, and overwhelmed. Working sixty to seventy hours per week, giving all my energy to everyone else, and not paying attention to how I was treating myself landed me in a debilitating state—mentally, emotionally, and physically. I was a mess.

That was when I began my own journey toward understanding how and why I had turned out the way I had—the same journey you're embarking on now. At a deeper level, I found that everything I thought, said, and did (or didn't do) was the result of unresolved past wounds and the beliefs I'd acquired along the way. I didn't know how to deal with difficult situations and painful emotions as they were happening, so I stuffed them away, thinking that was the way to handle them. That's what everyone around me did. How could I know any different?

I'll be honest with you. It took a lot of work and commitment to transform that old life into the one I live now. It wasn't always smooth sailing, but using the processes I'll share with you in this book, I finally healed past wounds and discovered a new way of navigating difficult emotions as they come up. I now have a career that is exciting to me and a relationship that I'd only ever dreamed of. I feel excitement in exploring far outside my comfort zones. I've learned how to keep myself healthy, live in a place of harmony, and become adept at knowing when and how to enforce boundaries. I now feel capable and confident when facing difficult conversations, and can communicate my needs clearly. When uncomfortable emotions arise, I now know how to process them so they strengthen rather than debilitate me.

I don't tell you this to boast, but to let you know that you too can have a life you love. But first, you need to learn how to heal your heart.

I have experienced many different processes as I've sought to heal my own emotional wounds. I also teach different approaches to healing and use a variety of methods for one-on-one work with clients. I've come to realize that there is no "one-size-fits-all" when it comes to personal growth. This book focuses on mindfulness-based processes that I have found highly effective. I also teach other approaches that are equally effective. For other options to assist you in your personal healing and expansion, please see the Resources section at the end of this book.

The Good, Bad, and Ugly of Emotions

As human beings, we are meant to experience and express the full range of our emotions. When we bury uncomfortable emotions consciously or unconsciously to avoid the pain, we disable an aspect of ourselves that is required to be whole. Our journey as human beings is to develop a greater understanding of who we are and make strides toward greater evolution. To do that, we must be willing to embrace all aspects of ourselves.

Embracing all aspects begins with resolving past experiences that left an imprint of negative emotions and limiting beliefs— beliefs and emotions that adversely impact your experience today. These negative emotions are caused by unmet needs and unfulfilled desires. Left unresolved, they become buried and fester like an untreated wound. And if we don't learn to navigate new emotions as they arise, we end up adding more weight to our already overloaded baggage.

Emotions in the moment—positive *and* negative—are perfectly normal. We're human beings with human emotional responses. Our emotions and experiences are what create color and texture in our life. What kind of life would it be if we didn't experience love, joy, awe, and excitement? And, though most of us would prefer to stay on the positive side of emotions, our negative feelings are important to experience the fullness of life as well. They guide us, help us survive, and even give us the added push we need to stretch beyond ourselves.

It's reasonable to experience anger when someone violates a boundary. It's appropriate to feel sadness when we lose someone dear to us. It's understandable that we feel fearful when doing something new for the first time or when we are threatened. These are all rational, healthy human emotions as we experience them in the moment.

These emotions only become stuck in our systems and turn into baggage when we don't allow ourselves to experience them—when we choose to reject, bury, and avoid them through various means.

The Baggage We Carry

Baggage is a loosely-wrapped term for anything that prevents us from being able to move powerfully forward in our lives. Heightened negative emotions that are inappropriate or unwarranted based on something that has just happened are indicative of baggage tied up in the emotion. Limiting beliefs that you have about yourself, other people, or the world you live in are also baggage. In each case, there has been a build-up of negative emotions and beliefs based on past experiences, and this is what we call baggage.

This baggage can severely derail us in the moment. Unresolved emotions shape our responses to life pretty much every day and in every way. It's like a snowball rolling down a snowy hill. At first, it's not very significant. As it rolls downhill, not only does it pick up speed, but it also gets bigger as the accumulation of snow becomes compounded. By the time it reaches the halfway point or bottom of the hill, it's gained a level of momentum and mass that has the capacity to do some very real damage.

A negative emotion that we don't process works in much the same way. It begins with a single event at some point in time when we couldn't properly digest the energy of the experience. The event may have been huge and dramatic, or it could be an event that seems insignificant to us as adults, yet felt traumatic to us as children. We didn't know how to resolve the emotional pain we felt in that first experience, so we buried it. As we continued through life and experienced the same or similar emotions and similar events, we just kept pushing the pain further and further down inside us to avoid feeling it.

This was our initial coping mechanism. We never learned how to properly deal with our emotional bruises, so we coped by avoiding them. Those unprocessed emotions compounded over time. What was once anger in the moment has now become generalized anger or even an underlying sense of rage that colors how we view the world and all our experiences within it.

We've all known people who are pissed off at everyone and everything all the time. They walk around like time bombs ready to explode over the smallest offense. What about the people who are perpetually frightened and worried? They hesitate taking even the smallest step outside their heavily guarded comfort zones. The person who is afraid to love? The one who feels unworthy? The ones who are relentlessly cynical? Who feel hopeless and impotent? All are examples of people carrying a lot of baggage in the form of unresolved past negative emotions and limiting beliefs.

Compare this to nutrition on the physical level. In his book, *Free to Love, Free to Heal,* Dr. David Simon writes that if you consume more dietary fat than your body can properly metabolize, it will lead to blockages in your blood vessels and arteries over time, and ultimately cause a heart attack. Atherosclerosis is a physical example of how past undigested residues can interfere with the free flow of energy in the present. From a medical point of view, unhealthy saturated fats and dietary fats accumulate and create physical disorder and disease.

The same is true for an accumulation of toxic, negative emotions that we don't metabolize or digest. Sooner or later, that toxicity will take a detrimental toll on our emotional body.

Your heart and psyche are both continually striving to metabolize energy and information. Your mind works day and night, during both the waking and the dreaming states, to process your thoughts and experiences so the intellect can grasp or make sense of them. The unconscious mind works diligently to process our feelings and experiences to extract what we need for our personal growth—meaning, lessons, wisdom, and knowledge from the experiences we've been through—so we can release anything that does not support our growth and expansion. But sometimes, the unconscious mind becomes conflicted and can't figure out how to process an experience. Or, in the processing of an experience, the unconscious mind accesses existing patterns or strategies from the past that keep you from growth and expansion.

You know that a negative emotion has turned into baggage and become toxic when you experience it in a way that is disproportionate to something that has just happened in the present moment. It's when you drastically overreact. You're consumed by whatever emotion you're feeling, and can't pull yourself out of a full-on tailspin. Another way of recognizing baggage is that you tend to bring the same negative emotion to *every* interaction. This way of being may be so familiar to you that it's like the air you breathe. And because so many others live their lives through their baggage, it may even seem normal to you. While it is common, it's not necessary—or healthy.

Letting Your Baggage Go

A critical key to living a life of purpose and passion is to learn to live in the moment. Many of us spend way too much time ruminating about the past and worrying about the future because of the baggage we carry. Living in the past or future prevents us from being present in the moment, right now, where the beauty, love, gifts, and joy reside.

I wrote this book to share some of the processes I've used personally, in my workshops with students and working one-on-one with clients for many years. These processes can help you break free of negative emotions from the past that consume your daily life now: anger and resentment, sadness and hurt, fear and anxiety, guilt and shame. They will also help you let go of the negative or limiting beliefs you hold as being true about yourself, other people, or the world you live in.

The purpose of releasing negative emotions, unhealthy decisions, limiting beliefs, and baggage in general is to free ourselves of the weight and our self-inflicted obstacles. It's to drop coping mechanisms that no longer serve us on our journey. It's an opportunity to clear the slate and begin anew. It's the foundation that allows the person we truly want to be to emerge.

By clearing out toxic residue from the past, you have more capacity to experience positive emotions. Old negative patterns squelch a positive mindset and emotions. For example, you start falling in love with someone, and the resurfacing of old negative feelings about being hurt in the past causes you to pull away. Or maybe you feel eager to start a new job, but the memory of embarrassing past failures turns your excitement into fear and doubt.

When you learn to release and let go of the stuff that doesn't serve you, you create space. You're opening a channel where there used to be a bottleneck or constriction. Like a water hose, when you squeeze it tight, the water can't flow. But with an open channel, your energy and emotions flow freely. You can traverse and experience more aspects of who you are, because you no longer have so many areas that are shut down. You can actually be happy from the inside out. You can even feel happy for no reason. You feel a lot more creative, inspired, and confident.

We all carry past baggage to some extent, be it our own past experiences or junk that was passed into our DNA through genealogy. In his book *Super Genes,* Dr. Deepak Chopra discusses what's new in the science of Epigenetics and how "the memory of personal experience—yours, your father's, your great-grandmother's—may be immediately passed on." He further elaborates that "the fact that memory can be inherited isn't new in biology."

Regardless of where the baggage comes from, I can tell you from personal experience that there's nothing more freeing than letting go of anything that binds you to the pain of your past. If an old decision, belief, or emotion prevents you in any way from moving powerfully forward, it's got to go. Plain and simple.

Journaling

Many of the processes in this book involve journaling, which is one of the most powerful and underrated tools you can use, and one that I rely upon regularly. By putting pen to paper, you involve both the left side of the brain, which is our logical analytical side, and the right side of the brain, which is the creative, intuitive side. The act of holding a pen and writing on a page allows the two sides of your brain to work together to draw your thoughts, feelings, and memories out from your psyche and into a tangible format for closer review.

Through journaling, you can pinpoint and focus in on more details of what you're processing. It also enables you to go deeper. Journaling can help you move sequentially through past experiences and provide insightful, intuitive, aha moments that you may have overlooked previously. I encourage you to embrace the process of journaling to express your feelings and observations. Allow journaling to be a powerful and cathartic tool for unfolding different pieces of the process.

Self-Reflection:
The Cost of Negative Emotions

For this exercise, using your journal, take some time to consider how your negative emotions from the past might be showing up on a daily basis. For example:

- *Can you think of a time when your fear prevented you from going after something or someone you really wanted? Maybe you allowed it to sabotage your relationships or career.*

- *Can you recall a time when your anger or resentment got the best of you and you blew up? Maybe you said something you couldn't take back, or you did something that you were embarrassed about or regretted later.*

- *Have you ever felt as if your sadness or depression was holding you down, like you couldn't shake the dark cloud, somber feelings, and hopeless thoughts that were consuming you?*

- *Have you ever experienced so much shame, guilt, or embarrassment that you avoided putting yourself out there for fear of being laughed at or ridiculed or bullied by others?*

Take some time to contemplate this and then make some notes in your journal. This will help you begin to identify what you're carrying around that you may want to consider releasing.

As you journal about your experiences, remember that your journal is for you and you only. Allow yourself to be honest. Write with compassionate self-inquiry. Your journal is not for public consumption. Think of it as you writing to yourself. You have to be able to rail at God if you want to, and use language you would never use in public. It's your safe place to rage, reflect, and contemplate. Your journal isn't meant to be perfect. You just write whatever comes to you based on the questions of each exercise. You're not trying to write a brilliant, clever essay or come up with perfect solutions. The idea is to let it flow and just see what comes through. By doing this, you'll find yourself expressing insights far beyond what your thinking mind can produce. Just put the pen to paper and let it flow.

For your journaling and the other self-reflective exercises I'll teach you, it's very helpful to set up a specific space in which to do them. Make sure it is a space where you feel comfortable and where you can be undisturbed for periods of time. You can choose a certain room or corner, and set it up with candles, music, or art that soothes you.

I truly believe that the purpose of life is to love more, be happy, and evolve as human beings. Of course, we are sure to meet challenges and obstacles along the way. Sometimes we overcome them with relative ease, and sometimes we fall flat on our face. The nature of life is the ebb and the flow, the peaks and the valleys, the smooth terrain and the bumpy roads. The idea is not to eliminate challenge, because challenge is where we find our greatest lessons. Through our daily challenges and the things we perceive as obstacles, we develop new levels of wisdom. The task at hand is to learn how to move through our experiences—good, bad, and everything in-between—and to extract the lessons. To glean the wisdom from all of life's experiences and to utilize them to make better choices for ourselves in the future. There's no right or wrong choice in life, because no matter what we choose in any given moment, the lessons that we need will be waiting for us.

We're all spiritual beings having a human experience for a very short time. Every single one of us deserves to live a life filled with joy, love, happiness, and fulfillment. If we're willing to till the soil and uproot the beliefs and emotions that hold us back, we will reap rich rewards.

"You are here to enable the divine purpose
of the Universe to unfold.
That is how important you are."
– Eckhart Tolle

Self-Reflection:
Who Might You Be Without Your Baggage?

Pull out your journal and let's start envisioning who you might become once you're free of the baggage that holds you back. For you, it may seem far-fetched to believe you have the ability to be, do, and have what you want in life. For this exercise, don't restrict yourself to what you think is possible for you. Write about what you would love, even if it seems out of reach. Imagine yourself without fears, doubt, anger, or sadness shaping your thoughts and actions.

- *What does this new you look like?*
- *How does this new baggage-less you feel?*
- *How do you feel when you wake up in the morning?*
- *What is different?*
- *What sorts of possibilities are open for you now?*
- *Imagine yourself in life's challenging situations: How do you respond differently?*

2

Preparation for the Journey

*"When I let go of what I am, I become
what I might be."*
- Lao Tzu

Before getting into the nuts and bolts of personal development work, we need to set ourselves up for success by getting clear on where we are now in comparison to where we want to be. Next, we prepare to build the mental and emotional foundation for the person we desire to become. Anything worth building must have a solid foundation to stand upon, or the ground beneath will erode and eventually crumble beneath us.

If you set out to build the house of your dreams, would you build it on unstable ground, or would you opt for land that is solid and supportive? Would you haphazardly begin throwing the place together? Or would you take your time in pouring a concrete foundation? Would you carefully plan each room, taking into consideration your current needs and future desires?

Much like building a new home, we need to clear out and reconstruct ourselves. We must know who we are, where we came from, and where we are now, as well as where we're headed. Then, and only then, can we plan and act effectively.

To build this mental and emotional foundation, you'll need to take inventory of your current emotional life and any baggage you may be carrying in the form of overwhelming negative emotions and limiting beliefs. Once we've become aware of our emotional baggage, we can then embark on the journey of letting go. This is the necessary groundwork for transforming your life into your desired vision of yourself. Laying this foundation is so very critical. It takes some time and effort. To set you up for success, we'll be developing new skills, practices, attitudes, and perspectives that will support you throughout the process. Let me introduce them here:

Compassionate Self-Inquiry

In this process, your most important practice will be compassionate self-inquiry. It's not effective to just roll into your work with guns a-blazing and expect to blow up everything in your life. Mindfulness-based practices like meditation and compassionate self-inquiry help us to develop present moment awareness so we may clearly assess the past and better navigate the *now*.

You can think of compassionate self-inquiry as the field or *container* within which all the processes and techniques happen. It's an attitude of being kind to—and curious about—ourselves as we start turning over rocks and excavating whatever we find beneath. It's the same loving, patient approach you use when helping others.

Buddhists often speak of the word *maitri,* which means compassion. To have complete acceptance of ourselves and to have a simple, direct relationship with the way that we are.

Maitri is our primary attitude and approach as we venture into self-inquiry. This quest cannot be successful unless we commit to holding love and self-compassion in the forefront of our minds. Why? The passage will at times be rough with unexpected bumps along the way. We'll have intense challenges and are certain to come up against issues that we'd rather avoid. We will also have calm, peaceful, insightful moments, where we feel the grip of past upsets beginning to loosen a bit and see some light at the end of the tunnel.

Remember to be patient with yourself and present in your process. Don't rush down the path. Stay calm, loving, and compassionate with yourself when you bump into pockets of unresolved issues. Maintain the softness of an open heart and an open mind, as if guiding someone you love dearly—your child or your best friend—through a difficult time.

I used to be full of impatience, anger, resentment, and hostility. In fact, as far back as I can remember, fierce negativity prevailed in pretty much all my internal dialogue about myself and others. It was my leading attitude in external conversations and, embarrassingly, revealed itself clearly in my reactive behavior.

When I first began doing my personal work—the real deep work—I had a habit of meeting my challenges with a level of intensity that backfired on me with an equal amount of negatively-charged energy. As soon as I came up against a pain point, I lashed out like a wounded lioness. Whoever was in my vicinity would be on the receiving end of a venomous verbal lashing, at the very least.

If I was alone, I turned on myself with awful words and sometimes behaviors. My internal dialogue sounded like: "I hate you, you pathetic, weak, ugly piece of shit. You're nothing but a burden to everyone in your life. Your mere presence has ruined everything. You will never amount to anything and you don't deserve to be here. No one wants you. You should just

25

die already!" In junior high school, I went through a period of time when I began cutting myself because I loathed myself to the point I wanted to inflict harm. As crazy as it sounds, I enjoyed feeling the pain because it mirrored what I was feeling on the inside. It was the physical equivalent of my mental belief that I somehow deserved it.

That sounds intense, and it was. These voices inside my own head were my constant companions. The more I tried to deny them or fight against them or push them down, the more abusive I became toward myself and others.

It wasn't until decades later, once I began exploring practices for emotional healing, that I started to understand this harsh internal voice belonged to a part of me that was terribly wounded and had never healed. I began to approach myself with love, patience, and compassion, and my healing process slowly followed suit. It was like I'd found the key that unlocked the vault where I had been storing my pain. By the time I arrived at this place, I was more than ready to do whatever it would take to come out of it on the better side.

From that point forward, I made a conscious decision to work with those wounded parts of myself from a place of love, honesty, courage, and most of all *maitri*—compassion. Self-compassion is imperative as we go through this process and face things that are extremely uncomfortable from our past. It's important that we stay tender and loving with ourselves, allowing ourselves to explore our feelings, thoughts, and actions objectively—not running away and hiding, but allowing the baggage to come forth. Doing this allows us to really work with our issues and understand them in a tangible way.

Another Buddhist term I use a lot in this work is *bodhichitta*. *Bodhi* means awake, open, and enlightened. *Chitta* means heart or mind. Pema Chödrön is an American Tibetan Buddhist and teacher. In her book *The Places That Scare You,* she refers to *bodhichitta* as our own spiritual soft spot. We must make a commitment to come at this work awake and open in our heart and mind. To approach this work, we need to keep our hearts and minds open without shutting down. We must sit in our pain and uncomfortable past experiences without trying to fix things in the moment. We must simply stay present to what we're feeling in the moment and let it soften us.

Healing our heart does not come from resisting or avoiding our deepest pain and greatest fears. Healing comes from befriending them. From getting to know them like we would a new friend. Healing comes from leaning into our emotions and providing ourselves with a safe space to open up and pour out. We lean in to understand how and why we became who we are today so we can let go of the unnecessary self-imposed obstacles we've carried inside us.

Letting go takes courage. It requires us to excavate our deepest and most hidden underground terrain. It calls us to go to the very places that frighten us, the places that we forbade ourselves from ever returning. And this terrifies us.

But we don't go after ourselves with shields of armor and weaponry. We don't arrive with a sledge hammer and demolish the very walls we originally built to protect ourselves. Rather, we approach ourselves and our past with gentleness and honesty. We lean in with a level of curiosity, with an open heart and an open mind. We explore our innermost vault with the innocence and love of a child. Leaning into an emotion means to simply to be present with it. We allow ourselves to become aware of it. We just witness the emotion as it ebbs and flows and moves through us.

Self-Reflection:
My Level of Self-Compassion

In your journal, take a few moments to assess your current level of self-compassion. Using a scale of 1 to 10 (10 being extremely compassionate), where would you rate yourself?

Now, dig a little deeper using these questions:

- *What do you say to yourself when you fail at something? What would your kindest friend say to you in that same situation?*

- *When you look back at your life, how critical are you of your past actions? How would an open-minded friend view your past?*

- *If a small child was slow to learn something, how would you treat him or her? How can you apply that to yourself?*

Key Principles for Transformation

To prepare for the journey, it helps to understand and embrace the four principles for transformation. Without adopting these, you'll find yourself swimming in circles, unable to release what needs to be released to tap into your inherent power and potential.

Principle #1: Perception and Interpretation

As human beings, we experience everything through our sensory perceptions: taste, touch, sight, sound, and smell. As we experience something, it first comes through our senses, and once we become aware of it, then we interpret what we just experienced. This is how we create our reality.

For example, a small child touches a hot burner on the stove. This is an experience and it hurts. She perceives this experience as painful and interprets it as being bad. Then, she creates her reality to be, "Touching hot burners hurts, and is therefore bad."

Let's say a child is teased in school when he raises his hand to answer a question from the teacher. He hears words and sees facial expressions from the other kids. He may even sense the energy coming toward him. That is the experience. He perceives what is coming at him as ridicule. This leads him to feel embarrassed. He then further interprets this to mean that he is flawed, or perhaps even stupid. His reality from this experience—being teased in school, feeling embarrassed, believing he is flawed or stupid—is now that he isn't safe to speak out in public.

Note, however, that the child's perception and ultimate reality *could* have been different. Say, for instance, he felt pleased to get the attention of being teased. He then could have concluded that he was great at getting people to laugh, a natural comedian. Based on his interpretation, "I'm the life of the party," this could be his personal reality going forward.

We'll cover this in greater detail in the next chapter. For now, just remember that anytime something happens, we perceive the experience; we become aware of it and have specific thoughts or impressions, then we interpret or translate it internally in a certain way, which then creates our reality. It's important to understand that the way we perceive something will determine how we relate to it.

Principle #2: Cause and Effect

This is one of the primary laws of existence. Every action generates a force of energy that returns to it in kind. For every thought, word, and action there is an equal response or effect. In this work, it's imperative that we take responsibility for our actions, own our choices, and be accountable for the effects or the results of our choices. We describe someone who takes responsibility for their life as being "at cause." They realize their life is a product of how they choose to live it, how they choose to perceive it, how they choose to interpret their experiences – and the choices they make on a daily basis. Determining that you are "at cause" puts you in a tremendous place of power.

On the other hand, a person who adopts a victim mentality renders themselves powerless. If you believe that other people and external events are the forces responsible for the life you now live, what power do you have to change? When someone operates under the assumption that everyone is out to get them, that the world is a terrible place working against them and their lives have fallen apart because of everyone and everything else, we describe that person as being "at effect." They've chosen to operate from a place of not taking responsibility, of blaming everyone and everything else for the way that their life is turning out. This person chooses to function from a place of melodrama, rather than choosing to be a conscious co-creator of their life. They do not see themselves as being *at cause* for the results they are getting, but merely that they are the *effect* of other forces.

To be successful in any personal development work, you must be at cause. You must be a person who's willing to take responsibility in every moment and on every level of your life. There's no way around this. No one is exempt from the law of cause and effect. We only get to choose which side of the lens we're looking through.

As Michael Brown says in his book *The Presence Process,* "The only way out is through and the only way through is in." This asks us to take an honest look at how we're showing up in life. Are we consciously choosing to take responsibility for what we create in our lives, or are we blaming everyone and everything around us for how things are unfolding?

Principle #3: Mind/Body/Emotions/Spirit Are Connected

We've all heard about the mind/body/spirit connection. This is to say that the mind, body, and spirit are all interconnected. To these three, I would add emotions. We have four "bodies"— spiritual, mental, emotional and physical—and each of these bodies are intertwined. Every ancient teaching believes in this concept and teaches it in its own unique way.

We know that everything is made up of energy. Energy comes down from the spiritual body (this could also be God, the Universe, Spirit, or your Higher Self—whichever you are most comfortable with) into the mental body. From the mental body, energy then flows down into the emotional body, and into the physical body from there. When energy is able to flow freely between each of the four bodies, we feel healthy and balanced. When that energy becomes blocked in any of the bodies, we become unbalanced, irritable, and unhealthy.

Research has shown that the mind—or our thoughts—affects our emotions, and our emotions affect our physical body. As energy moves through the mental and emotional bodies, it bumps up against any baggage we may have stored in the unconscious mind in the form of negative emotions and beliefs. This baggage can cause not only mental and emotional stress, but also physical symptoms. In the same way, imbalance or illness in our physical body can affect us emotionally and mentally. For example, with a cold or flu, our body may feel achy and we might feel blue or cranky. Not feeling well in the physical body can also affect our emotions and contribute to mental stress or lack of clarity and focus.

All these bodies are connected—the spiritual, the mental, the emotional, and the physical. The point of doing personal development work is to clear out the baggage from each one of these areas, so energy and information can flow freely. We're opening a channel so all four of these aspects of who we are can be in a state of harmony. Lines of communication are flowing freely, everything is communicating clearly, and we're feeling solid, congruent, and balanced on every level.

Principle #4: We Take Responsibility for Change

Responsibility for change means we recognize that we are the only ones with the power to change ourselves. In society today, we've grown accustomed to quick fixes and escapism. To ease our physical, emotional, mental and spiritual pain, we take pills, get injections, and use our work, psychedelic drugs, food, sex, shopping, social media, and various other means of avoidance. We'll use just about anything to bury our grief, hide our shame, and ignore what's really going on in our lives.

But nothing else and no one else can create the change you seek. The power to overcome and move beyond your pain comes from recognizing that *you* are solely responsible for doing the work. We can't rely on others to tell us what to do.

No one else can take action on our behalf. There isn't a magic spell to undo what we've been through. It's totally up to us to take charge, show up eagerly, and remain accountable for every thought, word, and action.

Self-Reflection:
The Key Principles for Transformation

Use your journal to explore the four principles for transformation. Working with each cornerstone, one at a time, do some self-exploration.

- What do each of them mean to you in terms of the work you are here to do?
- Do you feel any resistance toward any of them? How so? (Remember to hold your resistance with compassion as you explore more deeply.)
- How are they showing up in your life right now?
- In what ways have you misused or misunderstood them in the past?
- How can you see yourself becoming more empowered as a result of your awareness and utilization of each of them?

Our Commitments

The next piece of the preparation process is to make a few commitments. Should you choose to set sail, the voyage will be full of obstacles and bad weather. It's crucial that we understand these challenges are precisely what we need to experience so we can overcome our past and find the proverbial pot of gold at the end of the rainbow.

To embark on this journey, ground yourself in these commitments. A commitment is a contract we make with ourselves and, as such, commitment implies action. When you make a commitment, you dedicate yourself to a course of action you believe will result in the expansion of happiness and well-being. Commitment means moving through a door of change, a door you intend to close firmly behind you. In addition to practicing compassionate self-inquiry and being mindful of the key principles for transformation, here are the commitments I ask you to consider for this journey:

- Be fully present wherever you are
- Respond rather than react
- Be authentic
- Express yourself
- Abandon your comfort zone
- Honor silence
- Commit to your best self

The first commitment is to remain fully present in this process and your life. Showing up and being present, especially in times of discomfort, will enable you to find the healing you seek. Be willing to walk the path as it's laid out in front of you. Take every step and don't skip any parts along the way, especially when it becomes difficult.

All too often, people look for shortcuts so they can rush to the end of whatever they're doing. I'm sure you have plenty of examples from your own life where you rushed things and made mistakes and errors in judgment that cost you time, energy, relationships, and money. While a shortcut always looks appealing, beware; it's an illusion. Taking shortcuts leads to unwanted repercussions that will cost you more in the long run.

The second commitment is to focus on responding rather than reacting. You must make a commitment to take responsibility for every thought you have, every word you say—spoken out loud, written, or in your mind—and for every action you chose to take (or not take). Regardless of what's happened to you in the past, you commit today to take charge of how you move forward.

Look at the word responsibility as your "ability to respond." In this context, it means your ability to respond in a new way. Most people go through life in an emotionally reactive state. By taking charge, you pause just long enough to consider the consequences, good and bad, of your actions and behavior. Then, you choose to respond consciously rather than reacting without thinking.

The third commitment is to be authentic with yourself and others. As children, many of us were punished for telling our truth. We learned early on that finessing the truth to please others, spinning it in our favor, and sometimes even outright lying paid off. As you work through this process, it's vital that you be honest, first and foremost with yourself. Chances are, you've spent your whole life not being authentic and true to yourself in some way. As a young child, that may have served to protect you. Now that you're an adult, you know that hiding your feelings and past experiences is precisely what tethers you to your pain and suffering. Honesty is paramount.

The fourth commitment is to express your feelings and emotions. As you move through your process, you will undoubtedly come up against emotions you've long since buried, pains you forgot about, and issues you consciously believe you've already dealt with. You will access emotions and feelings that were carefully hidden from you in the past when your protective mechanisms sensed you weren't able to deal with them. Now, as those emotions begin to resurface, your internal systems may resist. You'll start to hear yourself say, "Okay, enough. I'm done here. I don't want to do this. I don't need to go any further." This is precisely when you need to hold strong, stay grounded in your commitments, take a deep breath, and carry on.

Expressing yourself in a *healthy* way is of utmost importance. It's easy to take our pain and frustration out on others, especially those we're closest to. How many times have you come home from a long day at the office and taken it out on your spouse, child, or roommate? That's not the kind of expression I'm talking about. Healthy expression can be done through writing, journaling, verbal communication with someone who can lovingly act as a soundboard without offering any response, or screaming and shouting—not shouting *at* others, but in a place where you're safe and alone. My former teacher and mentor, the late Debbie Ford, sometimes went into a room with a pillow and a bat. She expressed her emotions physically through shouting and hitting the pillow with the bat. This is a perfectly safe channel to express more intense emotions—provided you're alone and, again, bringing no harm to others.

You can also express yourself and your emotions through art, music, singing, dancing, or physical action and exercise. However you choose to express yourself is perfectly fine, providing you allow yourself to experience the emotions you are currently feeling in a safe environment.

The fifth commitment is expansion. Commit to abandon your comfort zone physically and psychologically. It's important to move your body through daily exercise and stretch your mind using the exercises, tools, and techniques provided throughout this book. Our emotions are stored as energy in both our physical body as well as our psyche. When we exercise our bodies and minds, physically and psychologically, it helps to move the energy through and out. Much like a baby chick who eventually outgrows the shell around itself, we too must expand and stretch beyond our previously constricted states to find the liberation we seek.

The sixth commitment is to honor silence as well as you can throughout your process. This doesn't mean you need to move to an ashram or boot your family out for the next several weeks or months. Rather, it's an invitation to create a safe, sacred place—physically, emotionally, mentally, and spiritually—where you can do your work. Silence is our greatest teacher. It teaches us about ourselves—what we gravitate toward and what we lean away from. We know that silence connects us more deeply to who we truly are at the core of being. It connects us to God, the Universe, Spirit, or Self—whatever label best supports your belief system. The more comfortable we can become with silence, the better we become at observing our thoughts and emotions.

Silence also connects us to the aspects of ourselves that hold our past experiences: the five-year-old child who was abandoned, the eight-year-old child who was ridiculed or bullied, or the seventeen-year-old who was told they would never amount to anything. Those are parts of us and not separate from us. They *are* us, and they're in desperate need of healing.

Throughout our lives, we've distracted ourselves. Whenever we've felt pain, we rushed to find ways to escape it as quickly as possible. Silence does the opposite of distracting us. Silence connects us, and that's precisely where we need to be to do this work, connected. When you're in your process of self-inquiry, silence enables you to be with the experience in a deeper way, which inevitably leads to greater transformation in the end.

The seventh and final commitment is your commitment to your highest and best self. It is your "Why." Why are you here?

Why are you choosing to step onto this path of self-discovery and healing? What is your commitment to yourself? What are you willing to do? Whenever we are working in the area of personal development, there will be changes we need to make in order to achieve the results we seek. Your why is your motivation, and it will be both your anchor and the driving force behind the work you do here. What are you willing to change, take on, or give up so you can finally be free from the past and create your new future?

Self-Reflection:
My Commitments

Take a few moments to rewrite these commitments in your own words with specific action steps. For example, you might write, "I commit to spending time in silence by walking in nature for fifteen minutes every day, allowing myself to just breathe and appreciate what's around me." Or, "I commit to expressing myself by being as honest as I can in my journal, writing down all the things I've never said to anyone—no matter how uncomfortable."

Are You Ready and Willing?

As you embark on this journey of self-discovery, take a moment to consider whether you're ready to go the distance.

Ask yourself, "How much do I want this?" Your "this" will be personal and unique to you; it's whatever you want to be, do, or have in your life. It may be a new relationship. It may be a successful career or family. It may be freedom from the past or finding your purpose. When we want to achieve a meaningful goal, we inevitably have to make some sacrifices along the way. Things may get uncomfortable, really uncomfortable, because we are called to give up something we may not want to give up. That sacrifice may be money you need to spend to go to a workshop or work with a coach. You might have to sacrifice a half hour of sleep if you need to get up earlier to do your exercises or meditate. It might mean giving up junk food or junk TV. It will inevitably entail giving up your reasons, which is a nice way of saying your excuses.

Becoming the person you want to be might even mean sacrificing relationships that are unhealthy, and it definitely means giving up many of the negative, self-sabotaging beliefs and emotions you've carried.

As you embark on this journey, the biggest question to ask yourself is: "What am I willing to give up in order to create the change that I so desperately need in my life?"

Self-Reflection:
What Am I Willing to Sacrifice?

As we've discussed, this journey will require some sacrifice on your part. In your journal, write down the types of sacrifice you think you'll need to make. Is it:

- *Time?*
- *Money?*
- *A relationship of some kind?*
- *Reasons and excuses?*
- *Beliefs that no longer serve your highest purpose?*
- *Certain activities or habits?*

Jot down whatever occurs to you. Now, looking at each item you've written, ask yourself, "Am I ready and willing to make that sacrifice?" If your answer is no, ask yourself, "Why?" Don't beat yourself up about your answers. Just take note that this is where you are right now, and make a commitment to come back to do your work at a time when you are ready.

There's an appropriate time and a place for doing your work. The road to self-discovery is said to be a lonely one for a reason, and that's because not everyone has the fortitude to go the distance and do whatever it takes to get out from underneath a lifetime of wounds. It's scary and it's difficult to stand up and face ourselves—and the world—as we declare that we're going to take back our life.

That said, it's very honest to admit, "I'm not ready." We can't force a wound to heal faster than it's meant to heal. My hope is that through the chapters of this book, and your own personal journey, at least the inhibitions to your healing will be substantially reduced. Should you choose to go the distance and do your work, I guarantee you will come out on the other side a completely transformed human being with a clear vision, open heart, and motivation to continue along your path of loving more and living greatly.

3

A Primer on Your Internal World: Your Emotions

*"These mountains you are carrying,
you were only meant to climb."*

- Najwa Zebian

To begin our journey into healing our heart, we need to develop a level of emotional intelligence. We don't need to become psychologists or earn degrees in mental health. We just need a basic understanding of how our emotions work and how to work *with* them. In this chapter, you'll come to understand what emotions really are and how to become more comfortable feeling them as they energetically move through you. You'll explore the sources of emotional toxicity.

In the next chapter, we'll get into how the unconscious mind works, review the origin of unconscious decisions and limiting beliefs, and discuss how our emotions, decisions, and beliefs become our overall story in life. Our primary focus in these two chapters will be on negative emotions, unconscious decisions, and limiting beliefs that keep our story from being the one we long to live.

Emotions

Emotions are simply energy in motion. The word *emotion* gives a clue to its nature: *e*-motion, energy in motion. If our emotions are made up of energy in motion, it follows that our emotions are also movable, changeable, and transmutable. Understanding upfront that emotions are the felt perception of energy in motion is, quite possibly, one of the most powerful concepts that we can understand. If emotions are energy that is in constant motion, that means emotions have the capability of changing instantaneously.

Many people misunderstand this and think that they *are* their emotions. "I am angry." "I am depressed." "I am sad." When one has an accumulation of past negative emotions from prior experiences, they go through life thinking that's who and what they are. They feel bound to those past emotions and believe that is who and what they'll always be. But that isn't how emotions are meant to be interpreted. Emotions are the way in which we feel the energy of experience. They can—and do—shift instantaneously.

Have you ever walked into a room where someone was in an amazing mood? As soon as you walked in, their smile, laughter, and overall energy lifted you into a happier place. Likewise, we've all experienced being in perfectly fine spirits, then walking into a room where someone was in an awful mood and we immediately felt our own emotional state shift. That's energy, in motion.

Knowing that energy can shift quickly is a powerful knowledge and understanding. It means that emotions in general can be shifted or transmuted in an instant. We can arrive at a place where we no longer identify the emotion as being who we are:

"I *am* depressed," or "I *am* lonely," or "I *am* an angry person." We might be *feeling* sadness, we might be *feeling* lonely in the moment, we might be *feeling* angry at the time, but it's not *who we are*.

The next important thing to understand about emotions is that they are driven by our deeper-level programming, which includes everything from our basic instincts as human beings to our values and the core beliefs we've adopted as individuals. Our emotions are also derived from our needs. Once our basic survival needs of food and shelter have been met, our emotions are largely based upon whether or not we are receiving attention, affection, appreciation, and acceptance—and also the ways in which these needs are met. We'll get into more detail about this in the coming pages.

For now, it's important to grasp the basic concept that emotions are energy in motion and they stem from our deeper-level programming, which is tied to our values, beliefs, and past experiences. The nature of energy is to move, shift, and transform continually. When we look at our emotions, we can see how they do that naturally on their own. Emotions are always rising and subsiding, ebbing and flowing.

The 90-Second Rule

Research shows that, unless we add something to them, emotions only really last about ninety seconds. The flood of chemicals streaming through your body that you recognize as anger, love, fear, or sadness naturally dissipates after ninety seconds, *unless* you add thoughts to it or an interpretation that keeps the chemicals flowing. For example, say a truck swerves into your lane of traffic. You have the instant flood of fear. Within ninety seconds, the fear disappears *unless* you start thinking, "Oh my gosh. I almost died. What if I hadn't looked up just then? What if I'd ended up in the hospital? Who would take care of my children? What an asshole!" The fearful thoughts you added to the initial feeling of fear will keep the fear going. This creates a dynamic where the emotion triggers a thought, which triggers the emotion, which triggers another thought—and on and on and on. Dr. Jill Bolte Taylor, a Harvard-trained neuroanatomist who studies the brain, says, "When a person has a reaction to something in their environment, there's a ninety-second chemical process that happens in the body; after that, any remaining emotional response is just the person choosing to stay in that emotional loop."

Remember, emotions are simply energy in motion. The energy of emotion is triggered by thoughts, which trigger chemical reactions in our body. So, essentially, emotions are the energy of our thoughts translated into physical feelings or sensations.

Everything we experience comes in through our sensory perception. Whenever we have an experience, it will generate thoughts. "That was upsetting." "Ouch, that hurt." "Yikes, that was scary!" The energetic impulse of that thought then triggers the chemical reactions in our body. We're flooded with hormones in our bloodstream and body, and learn to associate the feelings with emotions.

When someone goes through a breakup, they may associate the physical sensation of pain in their chest as the emotion of sadness or despair. If someone has a bad argument that triggers anger, they may experience a physical sensation of tightening in their belly or jaw. When someone has an experience of nervousness or anxiety, they will most likely notice an increase in heart rate and perspiration. The physical sensation of feelings we experience are thereby associated with an emotion.

Our Emotions are Derived from our Needs

Abraham Maslow's hierarchy of needs theorized that once our needs for food and shelter have been met, humans have four fundamental needs: attention, affection, appreciation, and acceptance. Every single one of us has a need for those four things. These are the fundamental needs we seek to fulfill on a daily basis.

Our emotions are derived from whether or not our needs are being met. Though we all have the same fundamental needs, we fill those needs differently. When we have a need for attention, how we go about getting attention will be determined by our current emotional state and how we have interpreted our past experiences.

From the beginning, we've been taught to seek what I refer to as the four A's—attention, affection, appreciation and acceptance—outside of ourselves. The problem is that we can never fully get our needs met by looking outside of ourselves, because the results are dependent on someone or something other than us. When our spouse is loving, we feel adored. When our boss praises us, we feel valued. When we spend money on material things, it makes us feel better in the moment. For our needs to truly be met, however, we must learn to fulfill these needs ourselves. In other words, it has to be an internal process—but we're not taught to do that. (We'll talk about healthy ways to fulfill our own needs in Chapters 5 and 8.)

When our needs are met, physically and psychologically, we feel comfort. We feel pleasure. We feel happiness. We feel contentment, satisfaction, cheerfulness. When our needs are not met, physically or psychologically, we tend to feel distressed. We experience pain, sadness, discomfort, vulnerability, moodiness. The moment we experience the discomfort of not having our needs met, we scramble to find things that will make us feel better. Nobody likes to hang out in that place of discomfort, so what do we do? We avoid it.

In our desperation to get back to feeling comfortable, where our needs are met and we're feeling happy, we stuff down the uncomfortable feelings—sometimes in very destructive ways. This avoidance of uncomfortable emotions is the beginning of emotional toxicity.

How Emotions Become Toxic

Unless we've been taught how to deal with our stuff—which most of us haven't—we avoid the discomfort by repressing our emotional pain unconsciously or suppressing it consciously. Once buried, we think it's gone away or that we've dealt with it sufficiently. Until it resurfaces. Emotional pain that isn't properly metabolized becomes stored in both our psyche and physiology. For example, something happened (or didn't happen) that resulted in not having our needs met. If we knew how to process the emotional pain of not getting what we needed, we'd be fine and the emotion could dissipate on its own. Unfortunately, most of us don't know how to do that, so the emotion becomes lodged within.

Over time and with repetition, that which has gone unresolved will fester and inevitably surface as deep-seated emotions like anxiety (with symptoms like insomnia), hostility, guilt, anger, resentment, shame, and depression. Odds are that you may be struggling with one or more of these deep-seated emotions, if not all of them. Most people do.

Another way of dealing with our emotions when discomfort arises is to become emotionally triggered by the situation and lash out. Quite literally, we go into a state of fight-or-flight, which affects our body, mind, and emotions. At a very primitive level, fight-or-flight is a survival response that's hardwired into our DNA. It's our body's survival mechanism, and it becomes activated whenever there's a perceived threat to our existence or the environment we live in. Of course, not all life situations are life-threatening—and yet, once the stress response is triggered, both our psyche and physiology will respond in whatever way we have been programmed to react. It may be physically throwing things around, fighting with our words, or retreating into avoidance. If we're able to process through the emotional upset, we'll find resolve. If not, we bury the emotions instead.

When we bury our emotions, we are saying to our unconscious mind that either we don't have the capacity to deal with them or we would rather pretend they're not happening. We try to escape the pain through drugs, alcohol, social media, work, television, sex, shopping, eating—any distraction we can find. By not dealing with it, emotional baggage becomes stored. In the fight mode, the physical body responds aggressively to a perceived threat which, in most cases, is really a series of unmet needs. Stress is how we respond to not having our needs met. If our needs are not met, we feel stressed out, and the physical body responds accordingly.

Take a simple example: Say that each day you go off to work doing a job you love. You enthusiastically contribute to the company's overall vision by collaborating with team members to improve the quality of products and service. You proactively come up with solutions to save the company money. Yet your peers disregard your contributions, and you're excluded from high-level projects. Your boss tells you how well-respected you are and that you are one of the company's top assets, yet you're overlooked for promotions and your ideas are constantly rejected. After a few years, you've become confused, sad, frustrated, and resentful. Your need to be part of a bigger picture, to be part of a collaborative effort, remains unmet. You've attempted conversations to resolve your concerns, but they haven't been addressed.

You feel stuck, like you have no choice other than to show up for work, do your job, and leave at the end of the day. Your frustration grows, but there's nothing you can do, so you numb your emotions through alcohol, television, exercise, or another method of escape. If you don't get out of the situation, your primary mode of operation will become one of hostility, cynicism, anxiety, or depression.

Self-Reflection:
How Have You Dealt with Negative Emotions?

Take a few moments to journal about your normal response to stressful situations and negative emotions.

- *Do you run away from them by distracting yourself?*
- *If so, what's your go-to distraction?*
- *Do you pretend it's not happening, that everything is "fine," and it will all disappear by tomorrow?*
- *Do you withdraw and hide out, giving others the silent treatment and retreating into your cave?*
- *Do you lash out verbally, in writing, or physically?*

Inception of Illness

Over time, not dealing with our negative emotions leads to the inception of illness. Doctors, medical professionals, and psychologists who are keeping up with current research would agree that more than 90-98% of our physical illness and disease comes from and/or is affected by mental and emotional stress. Due to our inability to resolve uncomfortable emotions, those emotions become stored first in our psyche and, over time, in our physiology.

Hanging on to stress causes an increase in blood pressure and stress on the heart, which contributes to coronary heart disease. An increase in sticky platelets in the blood contributes to heart attacks and strokes. The constant flow of stress hormones contributes to anxiety, insomnia, and addictions. The stress caused by unresolved emotions increases blood sugar, which contributes to diabetes and obesity. It causes a decrease in circulation to our digestive tract, which contributes to digestive disturbances. People under significant stress show a decrease in growth and sex hormones, which contributes to premature aging. Unresolved emotions also cause a decrease in immunity, which contributes to infections and cancer.

Stress affects our physiology, and that can eventually turn into long-term illness and disease. I find that to be wildly fascinating and terrifying all at the same time, because the stressors that contribute to our symptomology are, in large part, the result of our unwillingness or inability to process the emotions that result from our experiences. If we don't learn how to navigate our emotions and metabolize our experiences in the same way that our physical body digests our food, we'll eventually run into problems. That's why it's so important to not only resolve the past, but also to understand how to navigate the now and deal with emotional upset in the moment.

We also carry psychological seeds of illness. As I've mentioned, when our emotions are repressed, they become stored in our psyche as well as our physical body. These unresolved emotions ultimately lead to four major issues we see in our society today.

- Anxiety
- Hostility
- Guilt
- Depression

When our negative emotions are not fully metabolized, when we don't integrate them and digest them like our physical body digests food, we accumulate toxic emotional residue. The loss of a loved one, loss of a job, loss of a home, loss of an identity, betrayals, disappointments—all of these situations are part of life. They can be psychologically painful, and it's perfectly natural to feel distressed. But if we don't process and resolve the emotions from these traumatic events, we'll carry the emotion within the various layers of our being. The crazy thing is that we can end up storing multiple layers and, just like undigested food, they become poisonous.

How do you know if you're suffering from an accumulation of emotional baggage or toxicity? Some of the signs are consistent fatigue, lack of enthusiasm, generalized depression, complacency, heightened irritability, cynicism, and a high level of emotional reactivity. Identifying and letting go of our baggage, our emotional toxicity, is critical to our well-being on all levels.

Things like unfulfilled desires, poor lifestyle choices, and toxic relationships will perpetuate the fight-or-flight response as well. When the psychological equivalent of the fight-or-flight response is activated on a regular basis, our bodies are negatively impacted. For example, staying in toxic relationships—whether it's with lovers, spouses, friends, jobs, or family members—has the potential to plant serious seeds of illness.

Even things like watching too much television or constantly bombarding yourself with social media can be environmentally toxic to your health. You may be going on Facebook to avoid dealing with whatever negative emotions you're feeling, but doesn't it often perpetuate more of the angst, frustration, or fear you're trying to avoid? You tune into the news and get blasted with the latest conflict, economic problem, or political rant. When is the last time you watched a TV show that left you feeling better and more positive about life?

Psychological stressors can come from our environment, whether virtual or physical. Your workplace is probably toxic if you head into your office every day to spend eight to ten hours with negative people, demanding deadlines, and a demeaning boss. Maybe you are associating with a toxic community, a social or professional group that is constantly ranting about politics, finding fault with the world, or brimming with "impossibility thinkers."

What—and whom—are you surrounding yourself with? Have you chosen to participate in a community where everyone is focused on health, progress, and possibility? Or are you hanging with people who choose to gossip, complain, and rant about how messed up the world is? What is the environment when you visit your immediate or extended family? Is it a happy experience, or does it breed negativity? You have choices in the environments you live within. To avoid the inception of illness and disease, be sure you are choosing wisely.

Self-Reflection:
Identifying Symptoms and Possible Seeds of
Illness

- *Find a private, comfortable place where you will not be disturbed and can safely reflect for as long as you need.*
- *Set the energy, or the vibe, in the room. Light a candle, burn some incense, turn the lights up or down—whatever you need to do to "set your space."*
- *Take out your favorite pen and your journal, and open to a fresh new page.*
- *Make a list of any symptomology you are aware of currently. This could be something you're experiencing daily or sporadically.*
- *For each thing you list, take some time to consider what mental and emotional stressors you are experiencing in your life at this time. Make some notes about these stressors:*

  - *What is happening in your life?*
  - *What is the source of your stress?*
  - *Who is connected to this source of stress?*
  - *What emotions are you experiencing as a result?*
  - *What beliefs have you taken on because of the stress you're under?*

- *Next, see if you can recall the first time you became aware of your symptoms—the time when you first noticed there was an issue. Go back in time and trace what was happening in your life at the time the symptoms appeared:*

  o *What was the source of your stress?*
  o *Who were the active participants at the time?*
  o *What emotions were you experiencing as a result of what happened?*
  o *What beliefs have you taken on because of the stress you were under?*
  o *How long did this stressful time in your life last?*

- *Make some notes about how this situation affected you, and also how it is affecting you now.*

Secondary Gain

A secondary gain is some kind of benefit we get from staying stuck exactly where we are. It's how we benefit from holding on to our pain, limiting beliefs, or unhealthy behaviors. Whether it's money, attention, sympathy, or love, our secondary gain has become more important to us than being free of our pain and suffering.

Letting go of secondary gain can be scary, because it puts us in a place of responsibility for taking action in life. For example, one of my clients recently said to me, "I'm not sure I want to let go of my fear of being around crowds of people, because it keeps me safe." I asked her what would happen if people weren't out to get her and she was safe. Her response was that her parents would no longer need to be overly protective of her. They wouldn't drive her everywhere, order groceries to be delivered to her apartment, and pay for her rent. She realized that she would need to go out into the world on her own, learn to drive, and get a job. That was terrifying for her.

A few years ago, I had a client who had been in the military. She had PTSD and received money from the government because of it. When she realized that letting go of her PTSD meant she would no longer receive a monthly paycheck and that she'd be forced to take a job, she quickly retreated. She came up with a long list of reasons why she wasn't able to continue doing her emotional healing work. She wasn't ready to let go of her pain because she was getting paid to hold on to it. Crazy, right?

It's crazy, but not that uncommon. Many people wear their pain like a badge of honor. They've become intimate with it. It's been with them, or a part of them, for so long that it defines who they are—not just feelings they have from past experiences. This suffering has become their story, and they feel justified in holding on to it.

Letting go of that pain signifies a rite of passage from the old and familiar to the new and unknown. It can be terrifying to think about who we might become without our story. I've heard about this from friends of mine, family members, and clients—and it was also true for me at one time.

Take a moment to think about any secondary gains you may have and the benefits you get from holding on to them. For example, I was faced with the question of, "Who would I be without my anger, my resentment, and my choice to avoid being in a committed relationship?" I stayed safe by being single and independent. My secondary gain was that I got attention from holding on to my childhood story of abandonment. To let all of that go, for me, was terrifying. I could no longer point my finger at other people. Letting go would mean doing my work and being accountable for my own self-empowerment.

Self-Reflection:
Secondary Gain

Take some time to honestly consider the secondary gain you get by holding on to your negative emotions.

- *What benefits do you get from holding on to your pain, and from rigidly attaching yourself to your beliefs?*
- *Are you truly ready to shed anything that keeps you tethered to the past?*
- *What would it mean if you let go?*
- *What might be required so you can let go?*

4

Your Internal World: The Unconscious

"We read the world wrong, and say that it deceives us."

- Tagore

How Your Unconscious Mind Works

In understanding your own emotional toxicity, it helps to know a little bit about the unconscious mind. Why? Because the unconscious mind is where your emotional baggage is stored. So, let's cover a few basics. (I use the term *unconscious* mind, which others may call the *subconscious* mind. If you prefer the term *subconscious*, simply substitute that in your mind wherever I use *unconscious* mind.)

Your unconscious mind has several prime directives, or job descriptions. To start, the unconscious mind is the domain of emotions. This isn't to say you don't experience your emotions consciously. What it does mean is that there are times when you cannot consciously control your emotions, because they reside in the unconscious realm. For example, have you ever thought something was hilarious and were on the verge of laughing out loud, but you knew it was inappropriate at the time? Then, the emotion became so overwhelming you burst into laughter? You couldn't control the laughter consciously, even though you tried desperately, because the energy of the emotion was in the unconscious. Another example might be when you were consumed by anger in the heat of the moment, and as much as you wanted to control yourself in the situation, you blew up. You just couldn't control it because it was too overwhelming. The point here is that our emotions are located in the unconscious mind, and this is why we aren't always able to control them.

Another main function of the unconscious is to store and organize all your memories. Your unconscious mind links, categorizes, and stores similar experiences together, such as "sad experiences of breakups" or "all the times and ways in which I've failed." It also decides which memories (and the emotions attached to them) to hide from you. If your unconscious senses that remembering the emotional component of certain incidents would be too painful for you to re-experience, it might hide them in deep corners of your psyche until it feels you can handle them.

The good news is that the unconscious mind will present repressed memories for resolution when the individual is ready to release the emotional aspect. Many of my clients and people who come to my live trainings have arrived at a place in their lives where they are ready to resolve their emotional baggage, and this is largely because their unconscious mind has also arrived at a point in time where it believes they're ready to let go of the past. Your unconscious literally knows where all your skeletons are hidden. This makes your unconscious mind a very powerful ally when it comes to releasing your past baggage and healing your heart.

It's All in Your Perception

Emotional baggage doesn't necessarily come from events that occurred, but from your *perception and interpretation of what happened*. In a sense, what we remember as experiences never really happened—at least, not exactly as we remembered them. The reason is because our experiences are filtered through the ways in which we perceive and interpret, or make sense of things. The facts may be accurate, but the interpretations we made have painted a picture that contains so much more than just the facts. Two people can have the exact same experience, yet they may perceive it differently, have different emotional responses, and come up with different interpretations, beliefs, and decisions. Some people will end up with a truckload of baggage. Others with the same set of "facts" may not.

For example, two teenagers might not understand something that's being taught in the classroom. One teenager might feel fear, anger, or frustration in that situation, and shut down. The other teenager might feel curious, intrigued, or even excited and raise her hand to ask for further clarification. One is feeling like she's not getting her needs met, the other one is creating an experience of getting her needs met. It's not about what happened, per se. It's about how they perceived their experience, interpreted it, and absorbed it into themselves. We each think of our experiences as true. But our truth is based merely on our perception and interpretation of the experience.

Another example I use when teaching is the story of two sisters. They were physically, mentally, and emotionally abused by their father growing up. One sister overcame it, becoming wildly successful and acting as an advocate for others who had been through a similar experience. The other sister became a drug addict and was homeless, living under a bridge somewhere.

These twin sisters were both interviewed and asked, "How is it that you ended up the person that you are today?" They each responded exactly the same: "How could you expect, based on everything that I've been through, that I could have turned out any differently?" They both may have gone through the same experience, and perhaps perceived their upbringing as abusive. But the meanings they gave that experience were totally different.

One sister chose to see it as a call to tap into a deeper strength. The other chose to see it as the reason she would never make it. One sister chose to defy the odds to become a well-integrated, balanced, successful, congruent human being. The other sister became a mess, using her difficult childhood to define herself ever after.

Our job here, in this work, is to go in and separate the pain from the story, remove the charge from the limiting decisions and beliefs, and eliminate the unconscious decisions we've made that no longer serve our highest good.

Emotional Toxicity: Limiting Beliefs

Another source of emotional toxicity is limiting beliefs. Beliefs are any opinions or attitudes that we hold as being real or true about ourselves, other people, and the world we live in. *Limiting* beliefs are any beliefs and decisions that restrict or hold you back. Yale surgeon Dr. Bernie S. Siegel, author of the best-selling book *Love, Medicine and Miracles*, says that people are addicted to their beliefs. This is why, when you try to change someone's belief, they act like an addict. They swear the belief is not a mere belief but the *truth*. The question is not whether that belief or decision is true. For our purposes, the important measure is: *Does that belief support me in who I want to be, what I want to do, or what I want to have in my life?*

Let me offer a simple example. What if you walked into a job interview with the belief that you are an incredibly savvy, interesting, competent person with a lot to offer? What kind of interview do you think you'll have when you come in with that level of confidence? On the flip side, what if you walk into that same interview firmly believing that you're not experienced enough for the job and this company probably won't want to hire you? I'm not saying that you're guaranteed to get the job with the more positive belief. I'm saying that your negative belief is an unnecessary obstacle that has the potential of derailing and preventing you from achieving what you want. In other words, it's baggage that doesn't serve you.

Of course, not all beliefs are limiting beliefs. We have all sorts of beliefs that are called core beliefs. These are beliefs we have about something because we've seen it to be true in our reality. "Grandma is nurturing." "I can do anything!" "Love feels good." Many of our beliefs are favorable and even supportive. A belief is only *limiting* when it prevents us in some way or holds us back. Those are the beliefs we want to investigate and release.

Before elaborating on the establishment and formation of limiting beliefs, it's important to address the concept of thresholds. A threshold is a line which, once crossed, can result in making a negative decision and forming a limiting belief. What determines a threshold is both intensity and time. A person who has a single traumatic event may go over their threshold and quickly form a limiting belief, whereas someone else may have a slow build-up—a series of events that weren't altogether traumatic, but when combined over time, they created the same or similar limiting belief. How a person establishes limiting beliefs, then, is based on their personal threshold levels.

While our limiting beliefs are stored in the unconscious, like our emotions, we can have conscious awareness of them. We're aware of many of our limiting beliefs. They're not necessarily hiding out in the dark corners of our psyche. Rather, many of them hold a position that is front and center in our lives. They're the voices behind the constantly looping dialogue we hear running through our minds every day.

- I'm not good enough.
- I'll never find true love.
- I could never get that job.
- No one cares about what I have to say.
- I'm an idiot.
- I don't have what it takes.
- I'm too old.
- I'm not pretty/smart/educated/talented enough.
- I don't deserve it.

Unconscious limiting beliefs are subtler. They aren't so easy to pinpoint, because they've not surfaced as conscious thoughts. We're not aware of them and they aren't obvious to us. In fact, we usually don't even realize they're there. If we do have an inkling about them, we don't see them as being limiting beliefs per se. We see them more as *reality*.

This is precisely why they don't strike us as being personalized baggage. We see them as being a fact in our life. They look, sound, and feel much like the examples listed above as limiting beliefs, but unconscious beliefs are hiding in the deeper levels of consciousness. We may not know they are there, but our actions and reactions reflect them.

For example, a person may hold an unconscious limiting belief that she isn't capable enough for the career she wants. She pumps herself up with positive self-talk. She gets all the training and certifications her career requires. Then, when it comes time to interview, she forgets to set her alarm and misses the appointment. Or she fails to complete a simple application properly. Or she becomes tongue-tied during the interview even though she knows all the right answers. Her unconscious beliefs have sabotaged her efforts to actualize the career she wants.

Even though they have tremendous impact on us, we aren't aware of unconscious beliefs until we *become* aware of them. That's precisely why it's important to engage the unconscious mind when we're attempting to create lasting change. To do this, whenever we begin working with unconscious beliefs or emotions, we simply ask our unconscious mind if it's okay that we release them. It's simpler than it sounds. You simply ask the question and listen or feel for the answer.

Conscious or unconscious, limiting beliefs are notions we hold to be true about ourselves that formed when we were vulnerable. People told us things about ourselves that lowered our self-esteem, or we may have chosen to take on negative beliefs about ourselves without anyone specifically encouraging us to do so. We've all received negative messages directly or indirectly through parents, siblings, classmates, teachers, the workplace, society, or our own interpretations.

Because we had no way of filtering out these unhealthy, destructive beliefs, we absorbed them. First, we have a negative experience which leads to a negative emotion. If we're unable to resolve that emotion and make sense of what happened, we make the event and the emotion *mean* something about ourselves, which often turns into a limiting belief.

What if, as a child, your parents told you that you were a mistake? "You never should've been born. You're messing everything up. If you weren't here, I wouldn't have to work three jobs. If you weren't here, your father and I wouldn't be fighting." You might then absorb the belief that you ruin everything or that you're a burden in some way.

Maybe you were given away as a child. You interpret the experience as being abandoned. You create a belief that, because your parents weren't there and gave you away, you were bad or did something wrong. You expand on this belief: "I'm not lovable. My parents don't love me. They don't want me." By absorbing this belief—"I'm unlovable," or "I'm unwanted," or "I'm not enough"—it becomes a reality and shows up in every area of your life one way or another.

Self-Reflection:
My Limiting Beliefs

Using your journal, take some time to consider your own limiting beliefs and how they limit you specifically.

- *What are the beliefs you have?*
- *How do they prevent you from being the person you've always wanted to be?*
- *How do they keep you from doing things you dream of doing?*
- *How do they hold you back from having the things that you deserve to have?*

Ask yourself:

- *What are the thoughts that always loop through my mind?*
- *What are the negative things I'm constantly telling myself?*

Try to see these beliefs from a big picture perspective, and notice how these thoughts and beliefs are ultimately holding you back in your life.

Next, consider some of your unconscious beliefs.

- *Have you tried to change certain things about yourself yet found that, despite your best intentions, you've fallen short time after time?*
- *Have you noticed areas of self-sabotage (the hidden stash of cookies while you're dieting, falling in love with the same dysfunctional partners, spending money you don't have while trying to save up for something important, etc.)?*
- *Do you find yourself shutting down or acting inappropriately for seemingly no good reason in certain situations?*
- *If you could guess, what unconscious limiting beliefs might be behind this?*

To help you discover the source of a belief, you might ask:

- *What kind of person acts this way?*

This may help you identify the quality or characteristic you are emulating and reveal any beliefs you may have about yourself.

Emotional Toxicity: Unconscious Decisions

The third source of emotional toxicity is what I refer to as unconscious decisions. We make an unconscious decision based on an experience we had, but the crazy part is that we don't remember making it at the time. Our unconscious decisions always precede our limiting beliefs. We actually go through an unconscious process of making the decision to take on a belief. We just don't realize we do it because it is unconscious. And, we also continue to make unconscious decisions once we've already established a belief.

For example, I made an unconscious decision as a little girl that "I will always take care of everything myself." Because I was handed off multiple times as a young child, I ultimately created a belief that "I'm always going to be alone." I unconsciously decided that "I'll always take care of everything myself," based on the belief that "I'll always be alone." Our unconscious mind is simply trying to help us survive and avoid pain. But, though they originally served a purpose, our unconscious decisions tend to box us in, sabotage our efforts, and stunt our growth later in life.

In some cases, an unconscious decision may have a slightly different energy. In some cases, when an unconscious decision is present, there will be an automatic driver that sounds something like this: "As a result of this, I'm going to do—or not do (fill in the blank)," or "I'm going to have—or not have (fill in the blank) to avoid going through this again." Either way, it perpetuates a belief (and often several of them) and results in an unwanted behavior.

And we actually *decide* that we're not good enough, or we *decide* that we'll never be successful. Most often, we aren't aware of the decision because our unconscious mind is handling such things in the recesses of our psyche, usually in its attempt to keep us safe. At other times, our decision to take on a limiting belief is more conscious. We sort through the "facts" as we perceive them and come to a limiting conclusion: "My father left me. My last three boyfriends cheated on me. Clearly, I'm not enough and any men in my life aren't going to stick around long-term." These conscious and unconscious decisions and beliefs determine how we act or don't act in ways that might not line up with our stated intentions and goals.

For example, if someone has a limiting belief that he's not good enough, he made the decision to take on this belief, and he may also make a subsequent unconscious decision to stay small and unseen so nobody will ever know he is flawed. At some point later on in life, he may feel inspired to write a book, yet cannot bring himself to do it because of his belief that he isn't good enough and the preceding decision to remain hidden so no one will criticize him. If you have a limiting belief that you will always be alone because of childhood abandonment, you might decide to take care of everything yourself so you don't allow yourself to wind up in the vulnerable position of being rejected and alone again.

The real bugger about unconscious decisions is that we are always manifesting what we are most committed to at the unconscious level. You may think you are committed to your relationship, but if your unconscious decision is to always take care of everything yourself, you may never fully open up in the relationship because being vulnerable has the potential of landing you out on your ass alone. Again.

You know you're dealing with unconscious decisions and limiting beliefs when your life isn't reflecting what it is you say you want. You're stuck in a pattern that you can't break no matter how hard you try. You may even know that it's unhealthy to always handle everything by yourself, but the decision for this pattern—to avoid giving yourself fully and take care of everything yourself—is buried deep in your unconscious mind.

Knowing that we decided to adopt these beliefs—consciously or otherwise—is helpful, because we can use the decision point to trace the history of the belief.

For example, "If I stay small and unseen, I'll always be safe." You could ask yourself the question, "When did I decide that? And why?"

"Because of this or that, my life will never be the same." When did you decide that? And why?

"I'll take care of myself, so no one can ever leave me." When did you decide that? And why?

Of course, your conscious answer to these questions might be "How would I know when or why I decided that?" If that's the case, simply say to yourself, "If I *did* know, what would it be?" Then, listen for the answer and take the first thing that comes up. Taking the first answer that comes up is how you begin to communicate with your unconscious mind. If I were to ask you to give me a number between one and ten and you took the first answer that came to you, that is coming from your unconscious. This is the same voice you learn to listen to when inquiring about where your decisions and beliefs came from.

Self-Reflection:
Making the Decision to Believe

Take some time to reflect on the limiting beliefs you uncovered in the prior exercise. See if you can trace them back to an early childhood memory to learn when you decided to believe this about yourself using the questions above. By starting from the early memory, you can start piecing together how you became the person you are today. With knowledge comes understanding, and with understanding comes the ability to compassionately move through your healing process.

70

Components of Story Creation

The combination of our emotions, beliefs, decisions, ways we interpret our experiences, and memories are ultimately what become our story. Woven together into the fabric of our being, these are the things that unconsciously define us. This happens in approximately ten stages, although they all overlap one another and aren't always linear.

Phase One: Experience

As human beings, everything we experience comes in and is registered through our senses: taste, touch, sight, sound, smell.

Phase Two: Perception

We perceive the experience. Perception is being aware of, or placing our attention on, what just happened. It's basically how our impressions become thoughts about what just happened.

Phase Three: Interpretation

Interpretation is where we begin to decode the experience we just had. We try to make sense of it, to understand it. Essentially, we're attempting to translate how we perceived the experience, our thoughts, and impressions.

Phase Four: Evaluation

We also go through a process of evaluating our experience. Evaluation is a more refined version of interpretation, where we examine our interpretation of what happened and decide how to classify it. We're gauging it, considering it, weighing it so we might assign it an appropriate category. In the evaluation process, we decide whether this experience is good, bad, happy, sad, safe, or scary, and then we label it.

Phase Five: Labeling

Next, we move into the labeling process, where we assign a label based on our perception, interpretation, and evaluation. We now give the experience a label and know what to call it. We may label the experience as abuse, abandonment, betrayal, or neglect. If the experience is positive, we might label it as successful, exciting, or comforting.

Phase Six: Unconscious Decisions

Unconscious decisions always precede our limiting beliefs. Prior to taking on a belief, we make a decision to do so. For you to have the belief, you consciously or unconsciously decide this is going to be your truth. Again, some are conscious, but the majority of the decisions we make are not. Even our everyday thoughts, the things we believe to be true or factual in our lives, first began with the decision that they *are* true.

Phase Seven: Limiting Beliefs

Once our experience has been given a label, we decide to make it mean something about ourselves. This decision turns into a belief, and that belief is what drives our every thought, word, and action at the unconscious level.

Being given away by my parents multiple times in my early childhood led me to a series of limiting beliefs: "Nobody wants me," "There is something wrong with me," "I am a burden," "I will always be alone." A label of betrayal might turn into the belief: "No one will ever truly love me," "Men only want one thing," "Women cannot be trusted," "People in business will steal from me." I might make the label of neglect mean that no one's ever going to pay attention to me, so I therefore adopt the belief "I don't deserve attention" or "I'm not good enough." Note that each time a belief is established, it is first preceded by the (conscious or unconscious) decision to take on that belief.

Phase Eight: Pattern Reinforcement

Next, we seek to reinforce the patterns that have become so familiar. Speaking holographically, the unconscious mind projects our memories, emotions, and beliefs out into our reality for the conscious mind to experience. Generally speaking, whatever we believe or hold as being true is what we will experience in our daily lives. Pattern reinforcement is where we unconsciously go looking for the same type of people or experiences to reinforce our decisions and beliefs. You've probably heard the phrase, "What you go looking for, you are sure to find." Whatever unconscious decisions we've made and beliefs we've taken on, we now unconsciously attract that same type of energy because we perceive that as our reality—and, let's face it, like attracts like.

For example, childhood abandonment led me to seek friendships and intimate relationships with people who were not fully invested in the friendship or relationship. In my past intimate relationships, I attracted men who were physically and emotionally unavailable and who, from my perspective, "left" me in one way or another. They left me physically for long periods of time because of their line of work, and they also weren't connected emotionally so I felt alone in the relationship. Those experiences with men reminded me of my childhood abandonment and the memory-turned-belief that "I will always be alone."

In elementary and junior high school friendships, I attracted people who ignored me when I chimed in during conversations. I was excluded from invitations to parties and activities. One day we were friends, and the next day we weren't, then the next day we would be friends again. This back-and-forth reminded me of being given away and collected again. It created a lot of confusion and hurt for me. It also reinforced my belief that no one truly cared about me or wanted me around, that people I loved could not be trusted because they would always leave me, and that relationships weren't worth investing in because they never lasted.

Phase Nine: Gestalt Formation

Over time and with repetition, a gestalt is formed. I use the term "gestalt" slightly differently than it is used in Gestalt Therapy or Gestalt Psychology. For the purpose of this discussion, a gestalt is a way the unconscious stores similar emotions, beliefs, memories, and/or experiences. The word gestalt means pattern or organized field based on a similar property. In this case, the similar property is the emotional or mental label. It's how the unconscious mind encodes our memories and our emotions. A gestalt is formed after we've had a series of similar events that the unconscious mind links together. All our experiences where we were angry might be stored in one group or gestalt. All experiences of sadness can be stored in another gestalt. All experiences of fear or feeling afraid might be stored in another gestalt. All experiences of guilt and shame are stored in another.

I like to think of gestalts as the unconscious mind's way of creating a system for how it stores our emotions. As adults, our gestalts have already been formed. We've successfully found pattern reinforcement. We have now accumulated enough experiences of similar events, and we continue to add to those gestalts as we move through life.

Phase Ten: Story Creation

As we progress through life, our story is created based on what we have experienced as our reality, and we just keep adding to it. We registered our experience, which turned into a thought and led to perception. We then interpreted and evaluated what happened. How we evaluated the experience and the labels we chose to apply led to beliefs, which then ultimately move us into the ownership phase. When woven together, each of these phases or threads becomes the fabric of our story. We wear it as our reality.

A friend might point out to us, "That's not true. Life isn't this way." They've gone through the same process, but perceived their experiences differently. They interpreted things differently; their evaluation and the labels they decided to use are different. They made different unconscious decisions that may or may not have led them to take on the same limiting beliefs. The process of emotional encoding moves through the same phases, but we, as individuals, almost always come to different conclusions in the end.

Again, it's important that we not think of this process as being entirely linear. In some cases, one thing happens just prior to the next, and in several instances, the processes we run are happening simultaneously.

In the coming pages, we'll dive deeper into our own personal unconscious decisions, limiting beliefs, and negative stories as we begin to inventory our underworld. As you prepare to move into the next phase of your journey, please return to the commitments you made to yourself at the beginning of this book: your commitments to remaining open, showing up, and being honest and receptive to whatever you find. Recall your commitment to hold strong in your resolve and intention, and to understand yourself and heal through the process. This is _maitri_. This is self-compassion, and this is how we do the work.

5

Inventory Your World

*"Nothing ever goes away until it has
taught us what we need to know."*
- Pema Chödrön

Now that you've learned what emotions are and how they
lead to the labels we use and the stories we create, it's time to
inventory our own personal underworld, to do some digging.
It's time to bring anything that is preventing us from being,
doing, or having what we want to the surface, so we can do our
work of moving through our healing process.

How to Lay the Foundation

How do we lay the foundation we need to begin this journey?
It is a simple process that can be approached in many different
ways. There are no right or wrong ways to go about it. The
only wrong way to go about this work, other than to avoid
it entirely, would be to roar into it like some kind of sword-
bearing warrior hell-bent on destruction. We don't rush into
this work with the intention of bulldozing the walls we've so

carefully constructed and setting things ablaze. In fact, it's quite the opposite. Compassionate self-inquiry is the tool you need, especially as you dig deeper.

We learned about compassionate self-inquiry (*maitri*) in Chapter Two. Practicing *maitri* helps us stay gentle and patient with ourselves through the process. It won't serve us to push for instant results. We simply stay in the process for as long as we're required to be there, and we do so with an open mind, an open heart, and the desire to stay awake and aware of what we're moving through.

Before you begin this process, it's important that you truly have the intention and desire to create a new life for yourself. A life that's free of past baggage. A life that's full of possibilities, of inspiration, of health and happiness and love and fulfillment.

The process begins, first and foremost, with the understanding that for your life to change, YOU need to change. If you've found yourself living in a repetitive cycle where you can't find happiness, where you no longer feel inspired, where you've lost the feeling of passion about life, the only way to break out of that cycle is to first become aware of the fact that you're in it. You start by taking an honest look at what's got you trapped and then begin the process of unravelling yourself from it. Your thoughts, spoken words, and actions are what create your reality. If you want to change that current reality, it must begin with an awareness of how you are thinking, speaking, and acting. Ultimately, everything begins with awareness. Everything.

To embark on this journey, you must be willing to take responsibility for your thoughts, words, and actions. You must commit to showing up day in and day out, to participate in the process and do your work. You must stay focused on your intention to remain open, self-reflective, honest, and, most of all, compassionate and loving toward yourself and others. The first piece is having an awareness. The second piece is having an intention and desire to do the work, and the third piece is a willingness and a commitment to show up and *do* the work.

Self-Reflection:
Glimpsing Freedom from the Past

Start by taking a slow, deep breath. Hold it for a moment, and then let it out. Center yourself in your heart and just allow yourself to feel where you are right now in your life. Notice where you're carrying some wounds from the past, some residue of a previous experience that you know is no longer serving you.

Take a few minutes now to do some journaling about what you discover as you contemplate areas of wounds from the past. Ask yourself how those experiences still affect you today.

- *How do your wounds from the past still limit you?*
- *How do they affect your ability to love and to be loved?*
- *How do they keep you stuck in the past?*
- *How do you sabotage your opportunities, consciously or unconsciously, based on the pain of the past?*

Consider for a moment what burdens and baggage you're carrying. Imagine how you might feel if you were no longer tethered to the energy of painful relationships or negative experiences.

- *How would your life be different if you freed yourself from the emotional residue of hurtful episodes or the harmful messaging you received?*

Ask yourself these questions:

- *Are you ready to do whatever it takes to move through—and beyond—this?*
- *Do you believe you deserve to be happier in your life and have more success?*
- *Do you believe you deserve to give and receive love that's nurturing to the core of your being?*

Even though you may have some doubts, the fact that you're here reading these words is pretty good evidence that, at some level of your being, you believe you do deserve the life you've wanted—regardless of what you've been telling yourself.

Easing into the Process

To approach our most tender wounds and deepest programming requires a method that is both safe and effective. We must first identify the stories and beliefs that bind us to our unresolved emotions and past experiences. The key is to stop running from how we are feeling and take responsibility for how we show up in our lives. Becoming aware of our emotional states and repetitive patterns is the first step in changing.

Digging up our baggage is not a complicated process. Chances are, you have an area of concern on your mind already. Perhaps it's something that happened when you were a child. It may be something that happened several years ago, or something that happened last week or last month that is greatly affecting your mental, emotional, and physical states.

When you think about your history, you may feel some bitterness or extreme sadness around a certain experience. Maybe you have parts of your history you refuse to think about at all, or you feel the burden of some specific unresolved issue from the past. Take some time to consider things that have been difficult for you to navigate or resolve, regardless of how long ago they occurred.

Start by picking a specific experience from the past that left you feeling confused, angry, sad, afraid, jealous, or ashamed. Choose an experience that left you with a heightened sense of emotional sensitivity—something that infuriated you, or made you extremely sad. It could be the death of a loved one, a betrayal, being bullied as a child, or physical or sexual abuse. You may not want to start with something that was overwhelmingly traumatizing for you, but something else that has significant emotional charge. Remain open to the realization that it might even be something you think you've long since dealt with.

For example, when I began doing my deeper-level unconscious work with my teacher and mentor, the late Debbie Ford, I thought I needed to begin with healing from the tumultuous relationship I'd had with my ex-fiancé. It had been nearly a decade of my feeling abandoned and betrayed that reaffirmed my commitment to loathing men. Yet, what kept coming up for me was my relationship with my father. As a young adult, I had all but written him out of my life, and we'd barely seen each other or communicated for almost twenty-five years. I had done a lot of work around my father and his side of my family during my tenure at the Chopra Center. I thought I was totally over it. I had made my peace with the fact that we just weren't meant to have a close kinship, and I wasn't haunted by that in any way. I had no hard feelings toward my family, and I truly believed all had been resolved within me.

As Debbie began to probe into my heart and mind, it wasn't long before I realized I needed to sideline what I thought was my biggest source of emotional pain at that time (my ex-fiancé) and instead face my past with my father. I needed to resolve what I had long-since buried before I could heal the issues with the relationship with my ex. The biggest reason for doing this was that the two were linked to the same theme for me: abandonment. I needed to go back to the first event when abandonment took root as my theme.

The moral of that story is to remain open when it comes to where you think you may need to do your work and what ends up presenting itself. Remember *bodhichitta*: open mind, open heart.

Unpacking Our Story

To begin the process, we begin by unpacking the stories we've accumulated along the way, discerning what to hold on to and what to let go of.

Our story is like the trunk we carry, with all our belongings tucked safely away inside. Our stories are a composite of our core values, past experiences, emotions, beliefs, personas, memories, and a series of patterns and themes that we repeat unconsciously. Our stories are very real to us because they are born from our experiences.

Your story only becomes a problem when there is unresolved baggage from your past and you identify with it to the extent that it's who you think you are. We tend to believe our fate is set in stone based on what's happened in the past. I hear this in almost every conversation I have with people who are dealing with emotional upset. They believe they *are* their story versus being the person who had a series of experiences. They believe they'll carry whatever mistakes they made in the past into the future, and they may rigidly hold on to the belief that they *are* that failed relationship or missed opportunity they let slip away.

It all begins with an experience that generated thoughts and feelings that turned into beliefs, which have now become the way we see ourselves and the world we live in. When we get caught up in a reality that seems real to us because it's the only thing we know, we end up living in our pain and suffering, feeling like there's no way out. It's become who we (think we) are. But that is just an illusion. The experiences happened, and our feelings are very real, but they aren't *who* we are.

As we begin to unpack our stories, our objective is to go in and separate the emotional charge from past experiences, and come to know who we truly are versus the stories we have authored.

We often hear therapists, coaches, and mentors talk about the need to let go of our story—but again, the story itself isn't the problem. The problem lies in the limiting beliefs we've created as a result of our past experiences and the negative emotions embedded in them. It's not the story itself. It's the baggage we're carrying around that is associated with the story.

For example, a part of my story will always be that I was given away multiple times in my early childhood. What I had to let go of were the negative emotions and beliefs I'd created about what had happened: the beliefs that my parents didn't love me or that I wasn't enough. I can see now that my parents were doing the best they could from their level of awareness at the time.

Truth be told, I don't know that I would've done things any differently had I been in their shoes. I now have a healthy relationship with my story and have long since forgiven my parents. It's not about letting go of what happened. It's about letting go of old interpretations and beliefs. It's about pulling yourself out of the past where you've been stuck and unhappy for so long, and instead moving into a place of understanding and healing.

To let go of your baggage, you need to unravel it thread by thread, much in the same way that you created it—experience by experience. Imagine your story as a perfectly woven blanket that you've wrapped yourself in. Each intricate thread represents a time in your life when something happened: good, bad, happy, sad, scary, or safe. It has taken you a lifetime (or more) to weave together everything you saw, felt, heard, tasted, and touched. Likewise, it requires a process to unravel then reweave the threads of your experiences to create a beautiful new blanket. The good news is that it doesn't take a lifetime to undo it all; you just need a roadmap and some tools and to know where to begin.

Questions for Digging up Baggage

As we start to dig up baggage, the following questions will prove valuable. These questions help you move closer to seeing how your past experiences turned into the baggage you carry today.

Question #1: What happened?

Using the area of concern and the specific incident you uncovered, first ask yourself, "What happened?" As you do this, be very careful to just tell the facts of the story as best as your memory can support them. In this process, see if you can shift into a place of observation: seeing and recording the facts without creating any story around them.

When we go back into a situation or recall an uncomfortable or unpleasant event, we tend to relive the story, which gets us all worked up again. When this happens, we begin to judge ourselves and others, making assumptions about what we think really happened. We speculate about why the other person did what they did, what their hidden motives may have been, and why things unfolded in the way they did. We start to create a story of victimization or we berate ourselves for our past actions. It's important in this work to avoid going there, as it only perpetuates more of the drama we are seeking to free ourselves from.

It's okay to say, "My parents left me with other caretakers multiple times. My dad asked me to pull out my suitcase and I packed it. We drove and he dropped me off. Then he drove away. I was left there." That's what you want to write down—just the facts.

Question #2: What emotions were present during this experience?

What feelings were generated as a result of what was happening at that time? Write down specific emotions that were present for you during that experience. Make sure that the words you're using are actually emotions, and not language that leaves you in a place of being the victim (see chart below).

For example, I used to say, "I felt abandoned." "Abandoned" isn't an emotion. To get to the emotion behind the word "abandoned," you can ask yourself, "How do I feel as a result of having been abandoned?" In my own case, what came to me was that I felt sad. I felt afraid. I felt lonely. I felt full of shame, as if I had done something wrong. Keep asking the question: "How else did that experience make me feel?" You might say, "I felt betrayed by my parents," but again, betrayal is not an emotion. You could ask yourself, "How did I feel when I was betrayed?" Personally, when someone betrays me, I feel angry. I feel sad and disappointed.

As you work with the second question, use the charts below to make sure you're getting to the real emotions of that experience. Again, beware of setting yourself up as the victim in this story. When you use words that perpetuate disempowerment, you are giving away your power, and you're also making the other person responsible for your feelings. As we become more emotionally intelligent, we take responsibility for how we are feeling. We are then able to stand, once again, in our power. If you find yourself using the words on the first chart, it's an indication that you are using language that encourages victimization. It will serve you in both your current healing as well as future communication to learn what emotion is below the surface of those words.

Words that Perpetuate Disempowerment

Abandoned	Helpless	Put down
Abused	Hopeless	Rejected
Attacked	Ignored	Ridiculed
Belittled	Interrupted	Ripped off
Betrayed	Intimidated	Screwed
Blamed	Invalidated	Smothered
Boxed in	Invisible	Stressed out
Bullied	Isolated	Taken for granted
Cheated	Left out	Threatened
Coerced	Let down	Trampled
Cornered	Manipulated	Tricked
Criticized	Mistrusted	Unappreciated
Diminished	Misunderstood	Unheard
Discounted	Neglected	Unimportant
Disliked	Overpowered	Unloved
Distrusted	Overworked	Unsupported
Dumped on	Patronized	Unwanted
Hassled	Pressured	Used
Harassed	Provoked	Violated
Heartbroken		Wronged

Use the chart below to help you identify the feelings or emotions that reside beneath the surface of the disempowering words in the first chart. This is an integral skillset to develop for one who is cultivating emotional intelligence. You must be able to connect with and identify your emotions. This might be new for you. During our early developmental years, the majority of us weren't lovingly encouraged to identify how we were feeling when bad things happened. We were usually told to deal with it, or that it's just the way life is and get used to it. That carried on through our adolescent years and into adulthood.

Whenever you are searching for the deeper emotion, identify your state of being and ask yourself the question, "When I feel *overwhelmed*, how does it make me feel?" You may find that you come up with feeling as if you're spinning out. Again, ask the question, "When I am spinning out, what is the underlying emotion?" If you keep drilling down into each of your answers, you'll eventually arrive at an emotion like anger, sadness, fear, hurt, guilt—or some derivative of these core negative emotions.

In the following chart, I have noted words that reflect emotions in bold. The other words represent more of a state of being, though they do appear to have an emotional component. If you choose one of these un-bolded words to describe your feelings, be sure to drill down a bit further. For example, you may feel "self-conscious," but when you dig deeper, you may find fear or shame below it.

Emotions and Statements of Being

Afraid	Edgy	**Irritated**	Rattled
Agitated	**Embarrassed**	**Jealous**	Regretful
Ambivalent	**Enraged**	Jittery	**Remorseful**
Angry	**Envious**	Leery	Resentful
Anxious	Exasperated	Lethargic	Restless
Ashamed	Exhausted	**Livid**	Sad
Bereaved	**Fear**	Lonely	**Scared**
Bitter	Flustered	Longing	Self-conscious
Burnt out	**Frightened**	Lost	Shaky
Chagrined	**Frustrated**	Melancholy	**Shame**
Confused	**Furious**	Miserable	Suspicious
Cranky	Gloomy	**Mortified**	**Terrified**
Depleted	**Grief**	Nervous	Torn
Depressed	**Guilt**	Numb	Troubled
Detached	Hate	**Outraged**	Uncomfortable
Devastated	Hesitant	Overwhelmed	Uneasy
Disappointed	**Hurt**	Panicked	Unhappy
Disconnected	Impatient	Perplexed	Unsettled
Discouraged	**Incensed**	Pessimistic	**Vexed**
Distraught	Insecure	**Petrified**	Vulnerable
Dread	**Irate**	**Rage**	Withdrawn
			Worried

Question #3: What did I need at the time that I didn't receive?

Whenever we feel negative emotions, there is some need we have that isn't being met. In my example of being passed off in my childhood, my need was to be with my parents. I needed to wake up in my own bed and give my daddy a hug and my mommy a kiss. I needed to feel loved by my parents. I needed to feel safe in my own home and with my own family. With the past event you're working through for this exercise, be specific and identify what you needed that you couldn't get at that time.

Question #4: How did I perceive, interpret, and evaluate my experience?

As we go through the process of experiencing, the impressions left upon us lead to our need to translate what happened in a way that we can understand or make sense of. Take some time now to consider how you perceived what happened and describe how you chose, at that time, to interpret the situation.

Question #5: What is the limiting belief I developed as a result of what happened?

This is essentially where we begin to assign labels to the experience and make it mean something about ourselves which, in turn, becomes our limiting beliefs.

I made my childhood circumstances mean that my parents didn't love me and that I must have done something horrible for them to not want me. The limiting beliefs I developed as a little girl were, "This is how it's always going to be. I'm always going to be unwanted. I'm always going to be rejected. I'm always going to be alone. I'm always going to be on my own." As a result of these limiting beliefs, I made an unconscious decision that "I will always take care of myself so that I never have to rely on anyone else ever." I had additional limiting beliefs, including: "I'm unlovable," "I'm unworthy," "I'm not enough," "There is something wrong with me," "I'm a burden," and "I ruin everything."

Your next step here is to identify the limiting beliefs and any unconscious decisions you may have made as a result of this experience. The difference between the two is that a belief is static—"I'm not good enough" or "Nobody cares what I have to say"—whereas an unconscious decision implies action— "I'll see to it that I take care of myself" or "I'll stay small and hidden so no one can hurt me."

Question #6: How has this belief affected my life?

Now, go deeper. Ask yourself how that belief affected you at the time when you had the experience. How has that belief affected you since then? In what ways does it still hold you back today from being the person you're meant to be, from doing the things you need to do, and from having the things you want to have? Consider the different areas in your life and bring your awareness to how your beliefs have shaped your ability to give and receive love, achieve success, be healthy, and know that you matter—then do some journaling about it.

Question #7: What is the prevalent theme in my life?

In Chapter Four, when we went through the components of our story's creation, I shared how we go through a process of seeking pattern reinforcement. This is when we unconsciously go looking for similar situations, patterns, and themes that will support our deeply ingrained beliefs about what is true or untrue in our world.

As you've been revealing the ways in which your mind has labeled your experiences and the beliefs you took on as a result, there's a good chance you've started to notice a similar thread that runs through your life. Where else does this same theme show up?

Question #8: What reality have I created as a result of what happened?

You will recall that our story is a combination of all the components we covered in the previous chapter. Our story will inevitably create a reality—how we experience our everyday lives—that is the byproduct of everything we've been through. It will be a reflection of how we have perceived, interpreted, and evaluated our past. It will mirror our beliefs back to us and show us our fears, addictions, insecurities, and limitations through repetitive cycles and themes every day.

Close your eyes now and contemplate your current reality— the reality that is true for you based on your past experiences, memories, emotions, and beliefs. Open your journal to a fresh new page and spend some time journaling about the ways in which you can see how you created this as your reality over time.

Question #9: How is holding on to my baggage disempowering me?

In recapping all that you have dug up in this chapter, turn to another new page in your journal and begin to write down all the ways in which your baggage keeps you stuck in the past and prevents you from having the life you want and deserve.

How does it disempower your career choices or level of success? How does it derail you in the area of health and well-being? How is it affecting your intimate relationship? In what ways is it creating or adding to disharmony in your family or friendships? In what ways does it disrupt your religious or spiritual practices? How is it showing up on your overall life path?

Self-Reflection:
Unearthing Your Limiting Beliefs
and Negative Emotions

Now that you've worked through the questions for digging up baggage, here are some self-reflection questions to help you dig a little bit deeper and unearth more toxic emotions and beliefs.

- *How do you react when someone makes a critical or rude comment to you or about you? What is the primary emotion you feel in that moment?*

- *What do you reach for (think of your distractions) when you feel sad, disappointed, or lonely? What is the primary emotion driving your behavior?*

- *What is your first response when you're hit with a last-minute deadline or asked to take on more than your share of a project? What's the primary emotion you feel in that moment?*

- *How do you distract yourself when you don't want to deal with what's going on in one of your relationships? What are the emotions you bury by avoiding what's really going on?*

- *What do you do when you feel overwhelmed and don't know where to begin to get yourself back on track and into a healthy state of balance? Does this seem empowering to you or counter-productive?*

- *What thoughts run through your mind and what primary emotions do you feel when you sabotage yourself or others?*

- *How do you feel about yourself when you choose to stay in a toxic friendship, dead-end job, or abusive relationship?*

What If You Can't Identify an Event?

In my live events, people often share with me things like, "I don't know what the event is that caused this. I just seem to always pick guys who are no good." They know they're stuck in an unhealthy pattern, but they're struggling to track an initial or earlier event that started that pattern in motion. Alternatively, it's not uncommon for people to know what they need to work on and feel dissociated from the emotion. Meaning, they know some messed up stuff happened, but they don't feel any emotions around it; they can't access the *feelings* of anger or sadness or fear. Rest assured that it's as normal and natural to be able to identify an event and the accompanying emotions as it is to *not* be able to connect with them.

Fair warning: Your emotional baggage isn't necessarily like the family dog who leaps into your lap whenever you whistle. In fact, sometimes emotional baggage behaves more like your dog when he knows you're about to take him to the vet. He knows exactly what's about to go down. He'll hide anywhere and do anything to avoid going to that scary place. It's almost as if, at the unconscious level, our mind knows the uncomfortable journey we're about to take. Like our pets, who don't recognize the vet is trying to keep them healthy, our unconscious mind may not see that this journey is for our own good. It throws up walls to protect us from the pain and vulnerability we might feel when revisiting the past.

In fact, this was true for me when I first started my own personal work. I was attending a seminar and spent the whole weekend angry at myself and the process because I knew what I wanted to work on and couldn't access the emotions. I couldn't connect to my pain. It was as if a part of me was unconsciously conspiring against myself. Nothing was coming through, and I was frustrated as hell. I sincerely wanted to heal my past. I had pulled myself out of my job and my daily life. I'd paid for the hotel and the seminar and actively participated in every session. Yet, for most of the time, I just sat there fuming, convinced I would be a mess forever. This is an example of how our deeply our baggage has its hooks in us.

If you're not able to connect to an event that has substantial charge for you, a few things could be happening. You might be so blocked that it just won't come up for you. In that case, just ask yourself, "If I *did* know what event caused this issue, what's my best guess of what might it be?" Just go with whatever pops up for you. Even if you don't feel much of a charge on that event or you feel that you've already resolved it, go ahead and use it to run through the process. If you stick with the process, it will lead you to where that baggage is hidden. At the end of the day, not a single human being becomes an adult without having had some level of disappointment or loss or hurt, so don't let your unconscious mind fool you into thinking you're somehow exempt from having gone through difficult times—because it will try! You might have thoughts like, "Yeah, that happened and it sucked, but I don't really have any issues around it."

You could also ask yourself a few questions to get your baggage to surface. Ask yourself: "Who is it I want to *be*? What is it I want to *do*? What would I like to *have*?" Then, ask yourself the question: "Why don't I have what I want?" Or, "Why am I not being that person?" Listen for the answers and notice what comes up. Stick with it, feel into it, and let it lead you to the unresolved emotions and beliefs. There's some gold worth digging up there, I assure you.

Leaning into It

When you ask these questions—"Why am I not being the person I want to be?" and the others—you might hear responses like "Because I'm a loser," or "Because I don't deserve it," or "Because I'm don't have what it takes," or "I'm not pretty enough." These are your limiting beliefs. As you hear these beliefs, notice the emotions associated with them. For example, if you hear the belief "I'm a loser," lean toward the emotion you're feeling because you believe you're a loser. You might find sadness, shame, disappointment, or frustration behind that belief.

The questions above can be used to figure out what's driving us at a deeper level. As you move toward the emotions behind the beliefs, remember that emotions are simply energy, and energy is always moving. Every emotion runs its own pattern of peaking and dissipating. Energy rises and it subsides—it ebbs and it flows. Technically, it's the *energy* of the emotion that you are learning to lean into. Keep in mind the ninety-second rule from Chapter Three. This energy will keep moving if you don't add thoughts or beliefs on top of it.

The emotion arising is occurring in the present, and yet it stems from the past—during a time when something happened and our needs were not met. Our undigested emotions from that time are etched in our psyche. To lean into the emotion is to be present with it for as long as it takes to let it pass through you. Imagine the emotion as energy. Visualize it as something that is now moving through you, like a thick fog or clouds floating by; it's no longer stuck. Breathe into how you feel in the moment and let it pass.

A number of years ago, I went through a difficult breakup. It was debilitating for me. I had trouble falling asleep at night, and when I finally did, I'd wake up around 4 a.m. filled with panic, anxious about what I was supposed to do that day now that I no longer had that person in my life. Leaning into my emotions—my sadness, my jealousy of him dating other women, and my fear that I would be alone—enabled me to be present with them and to just "be" in it. I just allowed myself to cry, whether it was for three minutes or fifteen. Then, it would pass. I would feel another wave of emotion and repeat the process. Then, it would pass again.

This is what I mean by leaning into the emotion, just simply to be present with it. Notice it as a *feeling* you're allowing yourself to become aware of. Allow the emotion to move through you and just witness as it ebbs and flows. The more you can do this, the more present you'll become with emotions as they occur in the moment. In time, as you heal, they will dissipate more and more quickly. This is how you properly process your emotions so they don't become buried and cause problems down the line.

Beware of Distractions

During the breakup I previously mentioned, I remember pacing from room to room in my home, desperate to get away from the pain I was feeling. Almost frantic, I'd think, "I should go take a yoga class," or "I should go meet up with friends and just get out." But in that moment, I'd remind myself that those activities are distractions. They might be healthy distractions, but they're still distractions to *avoid* feeling the emotion. I made myself sit back down on my couch and just breathe through the angst, distress, and anxiety I was experiencing in that moment. I'd tell myself, "I love you. It's okay. We're going to move through this and be aware of every bit of it. Just breathe."

You'll need to be on the lookout for your own tendencies toward distraction and your patterns of escapism. As human beings, we prefer practices that won't cause pain or suffering, yet we so desperately want to heal. The healing comes from moving *through* the process, even when it's painful.

Think about it. If you sustain a wound and you don't treat it properly—or you straight up ignore it—it becomes infected, causing bigger problems down the line. Your mental and emotional healing process works the same way. If you bury your emotions, run away from your pain, pretend you're fine, and do everything *but* deal with it, it's sure to fester, showing up again and again. Each time, that emotional wound becomes more intense and unhealthy until eventually it creates physiological symptoms that have the potential of turning into illness and disease.

People often ask me, "Why do I keep having the same experience over and over again? Why do I keep landing myself in the same dead-end job? Why do I keep dating the same toxic person? Why do I keep having the same struggle with my health?" It's because you haven't fully released the emotions, integrated the lessons, or gleaned the wisdom from the first few times you had these experiences. If you had, you wouldn't keep doing the same behaviors every time you cycled back around to the next job, relationship, or health goal.

6

Releasing What No Longer Serves You

*"Without freedom from the past,
there is no freedom at all."*
- Krishnamurti

Once you've uncovered what has been holding you back or keeping you in negative patterns, you're in position to release it. In doing my own personal work, I've discovered many mindfulness-based techniques and processes to help with this release. I'm sharing my favorites here, the ones I've found to be the most helpful for me and my clients. All these processes are effective, but some may be more powerful for you than others. I suggest you try them all then continue to use ones that seem to work best for you and in different situations.

You'll probably notice that just by becoming aware of your toxic emotions and beliefs, they have less grip on you. Still, it's important to work through the processes to ensure that you've let go of those emotions and beliefs fully, and that you've gained the important lessons and wisdom from them. It's this important step that will lead toward lasting change. These processes can also be used for new issues that you encounter so they don't become trapped as baggage.

A note: Your unconscious mind hangs on to old emotions and limiting beliefs for a reason. At some point, it decided that you are safer with certain negative emotions and beliefs, so it may be reluctant to give them up. The first step in any release process is to get your unconscious on board with the release. This can be as simple as asking your unconscious, "Is it okay to let go of this old emotion, pattern, or belief, and for me to be consciously aware of it?" After asking, sit quietly for a moment and listen. If you feel resistance, ask you unconscious why it is resistant. You might hear that it's an issue of safety, or perhaps that you haven't yet gotten the learnings you need. You might need to negotiate with your unconscious mind by communicating with it in its own language. For example, if your unconscious seems to have an overwhelming fear of being in a happy, healthy relationship, you may want to remind your unconscious mind that the negative emotion of fear doesn't keep you safe. Get agreement from your unconscious mind that letting go of the fear and preserving the positive learnings will have a much more productive and healthy effect in the long run. For example, there may be fear as well as a belief of some kind—perhaps that relationships never last, or that all relationships end in pain and suffering. By identifying the negative emotion and its accompanying liming belief, you can converse with your unconscious mind in a way that soothes it—reminding it that it's okay for you to let this go now.

Technique #1: Personification

Personifying your emotions can be an extremely helpful tool for getting closer to what's really happening below the surface, and for extracting the lessons you need. Anytime we personify an emotion, we connect more deeply with the energy of the emotion rather than just thinking of the emotion in the abstract.

To personify an emotion means to visualize it and imagine it looking like someone or something we know, or possibly an aspect of ourselves. Personification gives us the feeling of having more of an emotional connection to it. Anger might look like your father or a ferocious dragon. Fear might look like yourself as a toddler or a little mouse. Your personification of sadness might be a grieving widow or a lonely ghost. The more you envision it as a person as opposed to an archetype or inanimate object, the more you can connect with it. When you personify your emotion, you make it more tangible, and your interaction with that emotion becomes more powerful.

First, identify the emotion you're working with. For example, jealousy was always a big negative emotion for me. As a little girl, when my dad left me, I assumed that he was going somewhere more important or spending time with someone who was more important. In my school years, when my girlfriends excluded me, I felt jealous because they all got to be together but didn't want me there. I wasn't good enough. In my intimate relationships, when someone cheated or left the relationship emotionally, I felt jealous thinking someone else or something else was better or more attractive than I was. I wasn't enough. When I sat down for the first time to work with personification, I identified the emotion I was feeling as jealousy. Once the emotion is identified, ask your unconscious if it is willing to release it. If you don't get permission to let it go, try using the dialogue I shared with you previously to have a reassuring conversation with your unconscious mind.

The next step in the process is to ask, "Who or what does it look like? Is it a version of myself, or is it someone else entirely?" For me, jealousy showed up in my imagination as a twelve-year-old girl. She was super skinny, dressed in torn tight jeans with unlaced high-top Converse sneakers, and a baggy white men's t-shirt with an unbuttoned flannel shirt. Her eye makeup was dark and smeared down her face. She had long, stringy, black hair and a really angry look on her face.

Your image may not show up as clearly. It might be something or someone that is familiar or something that doesn't make sense to you at first. Just go with whatever comes to you. If you stay open and curious, the image will get stronger and clearer for you.

After identifying the emotion and personifying it in an image, begin a dialogue with the person or entity you are envisioning. Invite that person or being to have a conversation with you. Ask the personification of your emotion, "What is the message I need to see, or hear, or get? What is it you're here to teach me? What is it I need to understand? Why are you here? What is this about?" If you stay open and patient, the emotion will respond to you.

In my case, I heard, "You've never paid attention to me. You've never taken care of me. You've never put me first. You've always put everyone else first and ignored me. I don't even exist." As I heard this, I realized this girl was an aspect of myself, a younger version of me that I had neglected for as long as I could remember. In every relationship I'd had—whether it was with my father, my friends, intimate relationships, or in the workplace—I always put myself last. My primary focus was on getting people to see me as worthy, valuable, lovable, fun, and good—all the things I believed I wasn't. By always putting everyone else first, I had made an aspect of myself jealous because I wasn't paying any attention to her. I wasn't taking care of myself.

After having a dialogue about what the emotion is trying to teach, ask how you can resolve the issue and what is necessary to reintegrate this emotion in a healthy way. "What do I need to know or do differently in order to shift the experience I'm having?" When asking this question, focus on the positive outcome. In other words, rather than saying, "How can I shift this so I'm not such an awful person?" pose the question in positive language. "How can I shift this so I feel better about myself?" Or, "How can I shift this so I take better care of us?"

The personification of my jealousy told me, "I need you to put me first. I need you to feed me properly. I need you to get rest. I need the choices that you make in every given moment of every day to support putting us first. I need you to choose friendships, partnerships, and job environments that take care of us, that we thrive in. I need you to stay out of environments where we're going to be battered, neglected, and abused."

With that answer, I realized what I needed to know and what I needed to do. I needed to shift my behavior. The lesson available to me in that moment was, "Holy shit! I've been ignoring myself my entire life because I was trying to prove my worthiness and value to everyone in the world. Look where that has gotten me." I reflected on my choices from the past and made some detailed notes about the lesson I had learned. I acknowledged that by neglecting myself, I'd ended up making poor choices. I'd ended up abandoning myself in favor of getting affection, acknowledgment, acceptance, and approval from others.

The next step is to integrate the personification of this emotion into ourselves through loving acknowledgment and a commitment to an action step. Change comes through action, not just knowledge. If you ignore the lessons of the past, they'll simply go into hiding again until their next opportunity to resurface is present. Rest assured, the emotion doesn't go away when you bury it. It becomes stronger and even more stubborn.

In my case, I apologized to the twelve-year-old me and said to her, "Please forgive me. I am so sorry. Thank you so much for showing up and for telling me all of this, for making me become aware of this." Then, I gave her a hug and said, "You know what? From this point forward, I'm going to take care of myself first. I'm going to be mindful about the friendships I choose and the relationships that I enter into, and the environments in which I place myself." I sat down and came up with some specifics: revising my work schedule, confronting a friend who'd been taking advantage of me, finding an exercise routine I could do more regularly. I put timelines on the actions I came up with and committed to doing them. I got serious about applying what I'd just learned.

The final step of the personification process is to journal about the conversation, to spend some time reviewing the conversation and learnings that come as a result.

Self-Reflection:
Personifying an Emotion
as a Form of Release

- *Begin with a few deep, relaxing breaths and close your eyes.*
- *Identify the emotion you need to work with.*
- *Visualize the emotion as a tangible person or living thing. Who—or what—does it look like? Describe in detail.*
- *Begin a dialogue: "What is the message I need to see, or hear, or get? What is it you're here to teach me? What is it I need to understand? Why are you here? What is this about?"*
- *Listen for the response.*
- *After having a dialogue about what the emotion is trying to teach, ask how to resolve the issue and what is necessary to reintegrate this emotion in a healthy way. "What do I need to know or do differently in order to shift the experience I'm having?" When asking this question, focus on the positive outcome.*
- *Listen for the response/message.*

- *Identify what the unmet need for this personification has been. What is the message or lesson for you here?*
- *Identify and commit to taking an action that will heal this aspect of yourself.*
- *Integrate the newly healed personification by accepting and honoring it as a part of yourself.*
- *Spend some time journaling about what came up for you.*
- *Take a new and appropriate action to respond to the unmet needs you uncovered and implement the lessons you learned from this experience.*

Technique #2: Become the Observer to Reduce Your Emotional Charge

If you feel overwhelmed by your emotions and are unable to move through the personification and/or forgiveness processes, you may need to start by reducing the emotional charge. When our emotions are too intense, they can prevent us from successfully releasing and integrating our past. This would be a good time to step outside the situation so you can loosen the hold this emotion has on you and then ease into your release work.

For this, you will use visualization, imagining yourself both in and out of the upsetting event following the steps below.

Self-Reflection:
Step Outside the Event

Begin by becoming fully present with the emotion you are feeling in this moment. Feel into it, breathe into it, and allow it to be a part of you.

1. *See if you can recall the last time you felt this way and what it was that caused you to feel or react in this way.*

2. *In your mind's eye, create a visual representation—a picture or short video clip—of the last time you felt this way. As you're looking through your own eyes, notice when the emotion was at its peak and hold the image there.*

3. *Next, imagine floating out of this picture and imagine that you are now watching yourself in the picture from across the room.*

4. *Now, play the picture or video clip forward until you gain a new perspective or feel that you learned something positive as you observed the situation.*

5. *Once you've gleaned the positive learning or gained a higher perspective on what happened, play the image or video clip backward, making each scene smaller and smaller. Dim the brightness and fade it out until the whole scene turns into a tiny speck and then disappears into nothingness.*

You will probably notice a substantial dissipation, if not a release, of the emotion you were previously consumed by. You may now go back and do the personification exercise or, if it feels appropriate for you, move straight into the forgiveness process.

Technique #3: Releasing Anxiety

Anxiety is a very real thing for many people. First, let's define what anxiety is. Anxiety is future-based fear and a negative emotion. Anxiety is what happens when a person consciously or unconsciously takes a negative experience from the past—including its emotional charge—and projects it out into the future. Can you think of a time when something happened in the past that hurt you or someone you know physically, emotionally, or mentally? Next, can you think of a time when the thought of that same thing happening, or worse, could potentially happen again to you or someone you love? These are times when people often experience anxiety; it's their fear from the past that they've put out into their future as a possible outcome. In some cases, the thing they're feeling anxious about may not have been a past experience, but rather their worry about what might happen. We sometimes tend to put the worst-case scenarios out into our future, and this can also create anxiety.

Another example of how anxiety shows up is when we are faced with uncomfortable conversations or big life decisions. When healing our past, a part of the journey is reconciling things that have happened along the way. For some, the thought of letting go of their story can be terrifying. Many of us don't know who we would be without the pain of our past. For a surprisingly large number of people, imagining what life could be like without our baggage is unfathomable. The thought of letting go can bring up fear and anxiety.

The point is that we create anxiety and worry by making an assumption about something that may or may not be happening—either now or in the future. We construct elaborate stories about what we think might be—or not be—happening, and then we convince ourselves that this story is true.

If you find that anxiety has its hooks in you to the extent you are unable to do the personification exercise or move through the forgiveness process, follow these steps to release the anxiety, and then go back to the personification exercise.

An important note: Your unconscious mind has a timeline that consists of your past, present, and future. This is how your unconscious mind stores your past experiences, memories, emotions, and beliefs. For this exercise, you will just imagine that you are floating above your timeline. To do this, close your eyes and imagine where your past would be if it was stretched out in a line below you. You might see it behind you, or get a feeling that it's off to one side—or you may sense that it's in some diagonal direction. Same with your future. Just imagine it; that is how easy it is to work with your timeline.

Self-Reflection:
Releasing Anxiety

1. Find a comfortable place to sit and close your eyes.

2. Become aware of your breathing, making each inhalation and exhalation slow and deliberate.

3. Bring to mind the specific event you are feeling anxious about.

4. Imagine in your mind that you float up above your body, above where you now sit.

5. Next, float out into the future until you are fifteen minutes after the successful completion of the event that you thought you were anxious about and stop there.

6. Turn and look back toward "now" along the timeline you just traveled.

7. Now, ask yourself, "Where is the anxiety?"

8. Now that the anxiety is gone, float back toward "now" and then back down into your body and open your eyes.

9. *To test to make sure it released, think about the thing that used to make you feel anxious and notice that there is no anxiety.*

Important Note: If the anxiety did not release, make sure you imagined the event completing successfully in step #5. Repeat if necessary.

Healing and transformation do not come about by staying stuck in our past. To truly be free from the bondage of our baggage, we must have a stronger desire to live our lives from a place of spiritual, mental, emotional, and physical health. Doing this requires that we let go of that which no longer serves us by whatever means necessary. Before moving on to forgiveness, it's imperative that you have released past negative emotions, received whatever insights or learnings you needed, and are ready to integrate the experience through the act of forgiving.

Technique #4: Forgiveness

*"Be assured that complete and natural
forgiveness is accessible to every heart, for
it is the nature of life to eliminate toxicity.
Given the opportunity and enough time, your
heart will release the uncomfortable feelings
generated from boundary-violating, need-
denying experiences but you must first create
a safe space for this process to unfold."*

- David Simon,
Co-Founder and Medical Director - Chopra Center

Another path to emotional liberation is through forgiveness.
If you truly want inner peace and to be free of the emotional
baggage that binds you to the past, forgiveness is a prerequisite.
You must not skip this step. Bypassing the critical act of
forgiveness will stunt your ability to be free from those who
have hurt you—including yourself. Like it or not, forgiveness is
often the entry fee you need to fork over to cross the threshold
into the life you want to live. As Gary Zukav wrote in *The
Seat of the Soul*: "An authentically empowered person is one
who forgives. Forgiveness is not a moral issue. It is an energy
dynamic. Forgiveness means you do not carry the baggage of
an experience."

What I've found in the years that I've been doing this
work, and in my own personal experience, is that the act
of forgiveness can wield a heavy hand for many of us. The
thought of forgiving ourselves or others is just too much to
bear, and we would rather hold on to our grudges than to free
ourselves of the cords tethering us to the past. The pain left
over after we experience a loss, heartache, disappointment,
or abuse on any level leaves a deep scar—an imprint in our
heart, psyche, and physical body. It makes perfect sense that

our basic survival instinct is to build protective barriers to keep certain experiences out and shield our most vulnerable aspects within. These walls are specifically designed to protect us from ever re-experiencing this pain. They are also the very things that prevent us from healing.

Why Forgive?

We learn early on that we can consciously choose to withhold forgiveness from those who have violated our physical and emotional boundaries as an added measure of protection. We believe that not forgiving others holds them in a perpetual state of suffering for what they've done. What we don't realize, however, is that withholding forgiveness binds us to that past experience. It shackles us to the unresolved emotional charge for weeks, months, years, and even lifetimes. At the end of it all, we're the ones who end up carrying the burden of what happened, leaving us with a heavy heart and unhealed wounds.

In some cases, you might receive a secondary gain from holding on to your story. For example, a person who was abused as a child may choose to hold on to that past and use manipulative behaviors in their adult relationships as a way of receiving attention or affection. I had a client who was in the habit of pushing her husband's buttons because it would make him lash out at her. Since she had grown accustomed to this form of attention as a child, absurd as it sounds, she found herself seeking attention from her spouse in similar ways. While you and I might see this as negative attention, she actually got the attention she thought she needed through this behavior.

Sometimes we refuse to forgive another person because we, in some way, believe that it puts us in a position of power, it lets us control the situation and enables us to protect our emotions. Holding on to our story in this way gives us the idea that we're right and the other person is wrong, and it makes us feel justified in our actions. We have to be willing to give up the illusion of these empty rewards in exchange for living our lives from a place of personal empowerment.

As an old saying tells us, "Holding on to anger and resentment and refusing to forgive is like drinking poison and waiting for the other person to die." If we hold on long enough, the seeds of illness that have been planted and the emotional constriction can eventually cause long-term physiological illness and disease. Not only that, but un-forgiveness will ultimately strangle our ability to trust and love again—leaving us old, bitter, and alone. You know those grumpy, old people who are super irritable and bitter and just no fun to be around? Odds are they are holding on to un-forgiveness and regret on some level.

Forgiveness is about lightening our hearts. At some point, we've all made choices that caused pain for another person. When we understand that we were all doing our best from our level of awareness at the time, we can gain a level of empathy and then forgiveness begins to unfold.

Getting to the Heart of the Matter

You will remember discussions from earlier chapters that our emotions, in large part, drive our behaviors, and our emotions are derived from our needs. When our needs are met, we feel happy, content, joyful, and at ease. When this is the case, we are more pleasant to be around because our emotions motivate us to behave in positive ways: doing nice things for others, engaging in social interaction, and going about life happily. When our needs are not met, we experience anxiety, fear, frustration, and sadness. During times of distress, we act out our emotional upset while searching for ways to avoid our pain. When we carry unresolved emotional baggage within ourselves, we filter our reality through memories of the past and are more prone to make choices that are counter-productive or even destructive. We've all run patterns of self-sabotage, and we've even gone so far as to sabotage others, be it through our thoughts, spoken word, or actions. In reacting to our own pain, all of us have the capacity to make choices that will, in some way or another, cause pain for someone else.

We each have our own story: our unresolved emotional past, our vault of memories, limiting beliefs, and a lifetime of experiences that led us to who we are today. Through compassionate inquiry and some specific guidance, we can learn to think about the person who hurt us and hopefully begin to understand how they became the kind of person who could do what they did. In her book *To Kill a Mockingbird*, Harper Lee wrote, "You never really know a man until you understand things from his point of view, until you climb into his skin and walk around in it." Empathy makes forgiveness more readily available to us, and we create empathy through understanding another's perspective and life experience. Did the person who harmed you have a difficult childhood or painful losses? Could they have been teased or bullied in school? Were they born with physical or mental limitations? What circumstances might have led them to make the choices they've made? And if you had been given those same circumstances, could you have ended up the same? Applying compassionate inquiry, even when just in your mind, has the power to expand your empathy and willingness to forgive.

Self-Reflection:
Forgiveness is a Heart-Centered Process

Bring to mind a person in your life who has created the most significant amount of pain for you. Maybe it's a good friend who betrayed you, a lover who left you, a family member who abused you, a boss or co-worker who took advantage of you. Journal about their story using some of the questions above. Add in whatever you know about their history. Where you aren't sure, just write down what you think may have happened. The point here isn't to have all the facts about that person's history. It's to bring yourself to a place in your heart where you begin to understand how they could have done the things they did. They probably did what they did because they didn't know how else to get their needs met, given their level of awareness at the time. If you had the same history, you might have ended up making similar choices, right? This can be true even in the most extreme cases.

Everyone is responsible for the choices they make in every moment. By trying to understand their motivations, we're not making someone right for what they have done. Forgiveness is not about condoning another person's behavior or letting them off the hook. It's about dissolving our own anger and allowing compassion and love to replace hostility, disappointment, and sadness so that we can be free. At the end of the day, we forgive because we deserve peace, and so we can once again return to a place of wholeness.

As you begin to feel more open and receptive from moving through this process of compassionate inquiry, check in with yourself and ask if you are ready to invite forgiveness to step forward from its hiding place in the dark shadows of your heart and mind. By doing so, you can experience the opening of your heart and a lightening of burdens, moving you closer toward the emotional freedom you desire.

It serves to mention that *reading* about forgiveness is one thing, and actually forgiving is another thing entirely. The act of forgiveness requires a commitment to yourself that you will—no matter how hard it seems—forgive the other person for what they have done. It is your commitment that sets the energy in motion to create a powerful shift. To have an authentic experience of that powerful shift of forgiveness, you must truly forgive in your heart, not just your mind. You need to take the action, not just read through this chapter. That being said, it's fair to say that you have to be ready to forgive. You have to want to let go of the past and truly forgive so you can be free to heal, trust, love, and live fully. If you feel you are ready to move forward with the process of forgiveness, continue on.

The following process of forgiveness can be done by journaling, visualization, or having a face-to-face conversation with another person. If it feels safer, it's perfectly okay to do this process in your mind or on paper without involving the other person. If this is new to you or if this seems particularly difficult or vulnerable, start with journaling it, then move on to visualization, and later to a face-to-face conversation if you feel that is appropriate.

I encourage you to forgive in-person whenever possible, if you can, as it opens up a channel for two people to move through the healing process together. However, keep in mind that you can't go into that conversation if your anger, sadness, and resentment are still highly activated. If you do, what you end up saying to that person will probably incite a not-so-favorable experience. If you haven't yet gotten to a place of releasing the intensity of your emotions, it's a bit safer to do it first in your mind. We can't ever know for certain how the other person will respond when we request forgiveness *or give forgiveness*. Even if you have released your negative emotions, it may turn into an argument if they're not in the same space. So, you need to be as calm and compassionate as possible when entering this conversation.

Forgiveness Process

To begin this process, create a safe space for yourself to do this work so your heart can be willing to open up and release the pain from the past.

Step one: Take a long, slow, deep breath in. Hold it at the top, and then slowly exhale.

Step two: Do whatever release work you need to do. You can use the personification exercise to dispel the emotional charge you feel about that person or event through self-directed conversation. If you are lit up and feeling an intense emotional charge, you may choose to use the process to step out of the event or the anxiety technique previously described. In less extreme cases, simply reframe; remind yourself that this person, while the choices they made conflicted with your needs, was doing their best from their level of awareness at that time.

Step three: Allow your awareness to become heart-centered and focused on your intention to forgive, trusting that healing and forgiveness are what you need most right now in your life so you can become emotionally free.

Step four: Bring the person who caused you pain to your awareness.

Step five: Reflect on that other person's story from what you wrote in your journal and imagine yourself in their shoes:

- Did the person who harmed you have a difficult childhood or painful losses?
- Were they abused or neglected?
- Could they have been teased or bullied in school?
- Were they born with physical or mental limitations?
- What circumstances might have led them to make the choices they've made?
- And if you had been given those same circumstances, could you have ended up the same?

Step six: In your mind and from a place of empathy, invite the person to come forward and thank them for being willing to have this conversation with you.

Step seven: Say anything you need to say to this person in your mind or your journal, so you can truly forgive them for what they have done. Because you are doing this process in your mind, you don't need to filter what you say to them. If you need to express your anger, sadness, or disappointment, allow yourself to do so. Maintain your intention to fully forgive, and keep the conversation focused on things that are necessary to say so you can let go and be free. You may also allow the other person to say anything they need to say to you so you can totally forgive them. This can be a powerful piece of the process. I do this part every time, and almost always hear something that softens my heart just enough for me to truly forgive.

Step eight: Tell the other person that you forgive them. Imagine, in your mind, seeing the other person accept your forgiveness for what they have done to cause you pain. Thank them for any lessons or wisdom you have gained from whatever happened. Next, sincerely ask for their forgiveness in return for whatever you may have done to contribute to the situation, or even for whatever ill feelings you've held toward them about what happened. This is an important step and one that some may find difficult. When forgiving someone for something they did to us, it may seem irrational to ask for their forgiveness—especially if we do not feel we did anything to deserve what they did to us. Chances are, you may have unknowingly contributed to what happened in some way or, at the very least, perhaps you wished ill thoughts upon them at some point along the way.

Whether you feel they deserved your anger, hatred, or wishes for karmic payback or not, it's important you ask for forgiveness as well. Knowing that we're all doing our best, even when our best isn't enough, we can only release the past completely when we can give and receive forgiveness simultaneously. Once forgiveness is received and accepted in both directions, it's time to bring it to closure. If it feels comfortable, you may opt to give the other person a hug in your imagination. If that's too much of a stretch, shake hands or simply nod in acknowledgment as you complete the process.

Step nine: Once you have completed this forgiveness process in your mind, you can help integrate the forgiveness by taking some kind of tangible action to heal your past experience. Consider if there's anything you need to do, an action step you need to take to be complete in your forgiveness. For example, you might feel the urge to write a forgiveness letter to the person who caused you pain. You might want to use your experience to help others who have experienced a similar pain by doing something like donating your time at a women's shelter or with the Big Brothers Big Sisters organization. Or perhaps you will feel more closure by doing some kind of ritual that marks your letting go of the past, like burning an old journal, watching a sunset with the intention of letting go of the past as the sun sets beyond the horizon, or just getting out in nature to clear your energy. This is a good time in your process to check in and see if anything else needs to happen for this wound to be healed and complete.

Forgiving others is one of the most courageous acts we can take on the path to emotional freedom and personal development. Had I not forgiven my father for leaving me in my childhood, I wouldn't have the amazing relationship I have with him today. Had I not forgiven my ex-fiancé for all he had put me through, I may not have opened my heart to loving and trusting again. I wouldn't have met the love of my life. If I had refused to forgive the man who violated my physical boundaries as a little girl, I wouldn't be a suitable guide for writing a book on emotional healing to help others on their own journey. These have been my lessons and gifts. It's up to you to find yours, and only you can decide if you will use them to grow and become a better person.

Self-Forgiveness

"Self-forgiveness is connecting with the need we were trying to meet when we took the action we now regret."
— Marshall Rosenburg,
Author of *Non-Violent Communication*

Up to this point, we've worked with things that someone else did to you. Because you're human, chances are pretty high that you have, at some point in time, done something that hurt another person. You made a choice that seemed to be important, good, or necessary for you at the time. But your efforts to fulfill your own needs left someone else's needs unmet. You weren't able to give them what they wanted, you violated their boundary, or perhaps you left them when they asked you to stay.

For some, self-forgiveness can be much harder than forgiving other people. We can't even bring ourselves to think about that hurtful thing we did. Sometimes, it's painful to face up to the choices we made. For example, say you were a bully in high school, harassing and beating other kids up. Today, as an adult and parent, you've outgrown that type of behavior. It might be difficult for you to actually think about what you used to do, especially if your own child is now being bullied. Or maybe you cheated on someone, not really thinking about the consequences. Your partner walked into the room and caught you in the act, and you saw the look of absolute anguish on their face. It might be hard to acknowledge that at one time, you were so self-absorbed that you didn't even consider how much pain your actions could cause.

In self-forgiveness, we have the same misunderstanding we might have about forgiving another. "If I forgive myself, that's like condoning the behavior, making it okay. Maybe I'll do it again if I forgive myself." Again, forgiveness doesn't mean condoning the behavior. At some point, you need to acknowledge that you're a different person than the one who did what you did in the past. When you forgive yourself, you're not condoning your past behavior. You were operating back then from your level of awareness at the time. Today, you have a different level of maturity and emotional integrity. Self-forgiveness is about taking responsibility for what you've done in the past and knowing that as you move forward, you can make a different choice. You can find ways to get your needs met that don't involve hurting other people.

So, let's now do the work toward self-forgiveness. Bring to mind a time when you know that what you said or didn't say, that something you did or didn't do, caused anguish or heartache for another person. Take out your journal, and consider what was happening in your life at the time. Make some notes. What were the needs you had at that time that drove your choices and your behaviors? What feelings did you experience at the time? Were you angry, frustrated, sad, or fearful?

As I said, you might find that self-forgiveness is more difficult than forgiving another person. Some of us feel overwhelmed with guilt, shame, and remorse for our past behaviors. We can beat ourselves up for an eternity over things we've done and the pain we've caused. My former teacher and mentor, Dr. David Simon, once pointed out that self-pity can also be a mask for self-importance. He said that some people hold on to and focus on their pain because they believe they are, unlike the rest of humanity, undeserving of forgiveness.

I will admit that, in writing this section, emotions of sadness, shame, and regret flooded over me as I recalled the way in which I moved out of my father's house at age fifteen. I shouted at him; I said scathing things to him that I could never take back. Then, I walked out, slamming the door behind me. A few years later, I wrote him a letter raging about everything I'd been angry about for as long as I could remember. In my mind, I wanted to hurt him as much as he'd hurt me.

As if that weren't enough, I wrote his entire side of my family out of my life. I didn't tell them that. I just disappeared. Nearly twenty-five years later, I got an email through some social media site from my aunt, telling me that my grandfather was not well. I'd just started my path of emotional healing, and I knew I had to go see him. When I arrived, my grandparents opened their front door and didn't even know who I was. That was how long it had been since they'd last seen me. It crushed me. I could feel my heart and stomach cave and it literally took my breath away. I knew in that moment I had come face to face with the repercussions of my past choices.

My grandfather was in a wheelchair at the kitchen table, unable to move his body, but he'd heard my grandmother at the door talking to this stranger—to *me*. She finally put two and two together and gasped my name. As I came inside the house to sit next to my grandfather at the kitchen table, I looked over to see tears streaming down his cheeks. I held his hand and I sobbed. When I was finally able to speak, I told him I was so very sorry for staying away, and that I could not imagine the pain and confusion I had caused. Between deep, shuddering breaths, I asked—over and over again—for forgiveness. My grandfather could hear every word I said, but he couldn't speak or move his body. He couldn't respond with anything other than tears. For him, they were tears of joy. For me, they were tears of anguish. I could feel all the self-loathing of my past rushing to the surface and I hated the sound of my own voice. I began to feel dizzy and thought I might black out. I just wanted it to be over. It was almost too much for me to handle. Then, my grandmother came around to put her hands on my shoulders and she said to me, "It's okay. Everything is okay; we forgive you and we're just glad you're here with us now. We love you, Tris."

They forgave me in an instant. Time had passed. Time that we could never get back. And it wasn't until I sat here, writing these words for you, that I took a time out, went to my favorite chair in the corner, cried my eyes out, felt into my emotions, and finally forgave myself for what I had done.

I forgave myself for ditching my family and for the way I treated my father when I was angry and vengeful. And when I was finished, I sat in my chair staring out the window into nature, feeling gratitude for having the tools and techniques to let go of the past, to heal and forgive—myself and others—and to gracefully navigate my emotions in the now.

We have all said and done things we wish we could take back. Now is the time for you to bring forth something you need to forgive yourself for. Perhaps you left someone who loved you dearly, even though they begged you to stay. Maybe you said or did something that caused someone else's relationship to end. It could be that you lied to, cheated on, stole from, or were in some way abusive to another. Whatever it was that you did, you deserve to forgive yourself and to be forgiven.

As you work toward self-forgiveness, keep in mind that life is about learning whatever lessons we need at the time. We wouldn't learn the things we need to learn if we didn't make certain choices—and mistakes—along the way. We evolve through trial and error. There is no such thing as failure, only feedback. You are a different person now than you were back when you did whatever you did. Your willingness to forgive yourself for the past demonstrates that you're ready to take ownership of your actions and make different choices moving forward.

The process of self-forgiveness is similar to forgiving another.

Step one: Take a long, slow, deep breath in. Hold it at the top, and then slowly exhale.

Step two: Do release work, such as stepping back into the observer role (Technique #2), anxiety techniques (Technique #3), or the personification exercise (Technique #1), to dissolve the emotional charge from whatever you did to hurt another person.

Step three: Allow your heart-centered intention to forgive yourself to flow through you, trusting that you are ready to allow healing and forgiveness to take place, so you can be freed from the past once and for all.

Step four: Bring your awareness to something you did that caused pain for another person.

Step five: Reflect on what happened. What did you do that created pain for another being? What was happening in your life at that time? What needs did you have at the time that drove your choices and behaviors? Acknowledge that you caused another person pain because your own needs conflicted with the needs of this other person. The only way you knew at the time to get your needs met was to do something that intentionally or unintentionally hurt this other person. What were those needs? How has this choice you made in the past affected you? How did it affect you then, how has it affected you since, and how is it affecting you now? Finally, what have you learned from this experience?

Step six: Get a clear image of yourself at the time you caused that pain for another. It might be the you that you were all those years ago, or the you that you were yesterday. Whenever the event happened, it was a *former* self who caused the pain. Invite this version of you to sit down and have a conversation with the you of today. Thank your former self for coming to this conversation.

Step seven: Say anything you need to say to this self so you can truly forgive yourself for what you have done.

Step eight: Tell your former self that you forgive you. Thank this self for any lessons or wisdom you gained from this experience.

Step nine: When you feel complete, give your former self a hug and imagine your two selves merging into one another, fully integrating into the newly healed version of yourself that you are today.

Step ten: If you feel that you need to take an action at any time during this process to feel complete and whole, take that action. You might need to contact the person you wronged to apologize and ask their forgiveness. Or, perhaps you write them a letter and then burn it. Whatever you choose, remember that this process is for you, not for anyone else.

If the forgiveness exercise stirs up emotional pain for you, take some time to breathe into how you're feeling in the moment. Remind yourself to come back to your intention to operate from a place of love. Revisit the emotional release techniques I've shared with you earlier in this chapter. Do the release work needed to clean up any residual toxicity.

Revisit the lessons, wisdom, or gifts that have been set at your doorstep as a result of all you've been through. Now that you've moved through the forgiveness process, you get to choose what to do with those learnings.

The Key is Surrender

Author and teacher Caroline Myss says, "Until you surrender the need to know *why* things happened to you as they did, you will hold on to your wounds with the intense emotional fire." She goes on to say that forgiveness is not an intellectual exercise. We may seek some understanding of the other person's motivations, but in the end, it's not about analyzing. If you don't first release your negative emotions, all the mental effort you put into forgiving and healing will be useless. She tells us that you must really put your heart into the process for it to be successful. She goes on to say "...forgiveness has nothing to do with the individuals who harmed you, it's the act of accepting that there's a greater map of life through which flow many rivers of events and relationships, all interconnected. Forgiveness is your release from the hell of wanting to know what cannot be known and from wanting to see others suffer because they have hurt you." The same applies for self-forgiveness.

How do you know if you've truly surrendered and forgiven someone? If you haven't really forgiven someone, you'll still have a heightened sense of sensitivity or emotional charge whenever you think of that person or experience. If you still feel hatred, a high level of anger, hostility, hurt, or resentment, then you know you haven't moved through the forgiveness process fully. This would be a good time to ask yourself if you are really ready to let go of the past and truly forgive. If the answer is yes, release your negative emotions and do the process again while remaining in your heart and coming from a place of acceptance and surrender. Lean into compassion and allow the process to resolve the past for you.

When you've truly forgiven, you can think back on whatever happened without feeling a charge. You can recall the emotions you felt, but you don't actually feel them rise up in you again. You're no longer plugged in emotionally. In fact, what you notice instead might be a thought of, "Wow. That was an unfortunate set of circumstances. Total bummer that it happened." At the same time, you can see how it had to happen so you could grasp certain lessons. It was necessary for your personal evolution. You can observe and witness that past event rather than react to it all over again.

Ongoing Process

This is an ongoing process. It isn't something that you do once and you're done. You'll be processing different emotions and maybe re-processing deeper layers that present the same or similar emotion in different contexts. The first time I used the personification process with my own jealousy, a huge chunk got released. Yet, I knew there was more that needed to be cleared, because it showed up in different areas in my life in similar ways. As that last bit of jealousy surfaced, I took myself through the personification process again and found a different image of the emotion to interact with. So, you see, there are many layers that comprise our mental and emotional bodies. Like peeling back the layers of an onion, it can sometimes burn with each new layer. Keep doing your work whenever new baggage arises, and you will find your load lightening exponentially. Your spiritual connection will be more apparent, your mind clearer, your heart more open and loving, and your physical body more energized and healthy. From here, with a clean slate, you can begin building a new life grounded in awareness, transparency, compassion, and inspiration. This is your new beginning.

7

Navigating the Now

"Breakdowns are your greatest breakthroughs. Rank the severity, and know this is the quantity of the spectacular gift you'll receive on the other side. You planned it all perfectly."
- Melanie Tonia Evans

Now that you have learned how to dig up your baggage, release it, and find healing through forgiveness, the next leg of the journey is learning how to navigate your emotions in the now. Our emotions are the number one thing that have the potential to derail us in ways that can be devastating—and sometimes irreversible. Knowing how to get a handle on your emotions as they arise in the moment is crucial if you hope to respond to life's curveballs in a way that helps you to grow and evolve while maintaining a level of integrity in how you navigate your experiences.

Have you ever had a stressful day and ended up taking it out on your coworkers, spouse, or children? We've all had those days when something goes wrong and it ends up derailing our entire day or week. Dealing with your emotions in a healthy way is how you can avoid creating new baggage. It requires a combination of awareness and mindset for more effectively managing life's challenges on a daily basis.

The tricky part is that it's not going to be the exact same process every single time for every single person. There are several ways to handle your boss' poor attitude, or deal with unexpected variables that throw off your morning routine, or contend with overwhelm and exhaustion that leave you feeling edgy at the end of the day. I wish I could give you a cookie cutter template that you could pull out each time you encounter some form of emotional distress. But it's just not that simple.

Each of us experiences life differently. We perceive and interpret things differently. Some people see the color pink as being salmon. Some people would call it red, whereas another person might argue, "No, that's a muted orange." Or, someone might say, "It's such a hot day outside today with these Santa Ana conditions," yet another person might say, "Actually, it feels perfect for me and the breeze is great." One person might say, "The comment so-and-so made today in that meeting was so rude and abrasive." Yet another person might say, "Actually, I really appreciated the fact that he got straight to the point and called it what it was."

Even the words we use have different meanings based on each individual. The word integrity to me might mean something completely different than what it means to you. This is why it's so important to have several approaches to cultivating emotional intelligence.

What I'm offering you here isn't a specific template or science, but rather a series of different approaches you can use for navigating your daily life experiences and emotions so they don't end up accumulating as more emotional baggage. These are not the only ways to handle upsetting experiences. They are simply some of my own favorites and ones I use regularly. Your goal is to use the power of your emotions to support what you want out of life, not sabotage your efforts and intentions. Use whatever works best for you.

Before we get into specific techniques and tools, we need to recognize that we're all doing the best we can based on our level of awareness at any point in time. No matter what's going on in your life, keep in mind that we're usually doing the very best we know how, given the circumstances and resources we have available to us in this moment. I say "usually," because it's likely each of us could identify areas where we know we're not showing up one hundred percent. This is part of the learning involved in becoming a more empowered and aware being.

We will be focusing on the present moment a lot in this chapter, as this is where the gold is at. It will help to stay consciously aware of limiting beliefs that occupy your thoughts and negative emotions that drive your behaviors. This will enable you to catch glimpses of how you react to certain triggers and also help you get the lessons and learnings necessary to move you powerfully forward in your life.

Before you get started with this process, again, also be on the lookout for your distractions. In Pema Chodron's book *The Places That Scare You*, she asks three powerful questions: 1) "What do I do when I can't handle what's going on?" 2) "Where do I look for strength?" and 3) "In what or whom do I place my trust?" As you prepare to move through the process of dealing with your stuff in the moment, stay aware of your distraction patterns so you can catch yourself and stay on track with the process.

Trading Old Strategies for New

It's safe to assume that few of us received formal instructions during childhood in how to process our emotions as they pop up. No one sat us down and said, "Okay, when you have your first breakup, here's what you have to do and in time you'll feel better." I'm guessing no one told you how to process that rejection letter from the college you wanted to go to, or being fired from your job. No one told you what emotions you'd encounter when you had your first child, going from a non-parent to holding a newborn child in your arms.

Unfortunately, we aren't given guide books for dealing with the emotions of life, and there's no one right way to do it. The only *wrong* way to handle our emotions is to *not* do it at all, to avoid dealing with things as they come up. To not deal with life, to check out, to go into trance, to pretend like "ignorance is bliss" means you're avoiding the very things you need to move through to become the person you're meant to be.

Because we had no formal instruction, the majority of us were left to observe our parents, caretakers, teachers, friends, and other people and how they all seemed to handle emotions. We observed and modeled the behavior of others, especially those close to us. "Dad lashes out when someone disappoints him, throwing and breaking things, and shouting at everybody. Oh, okay. So that's an appropriate expression of anger." If that's our childhood experience, that's what we may end up modeling.

However, it's worth acknowledging that the people we modeled may or may not have been altogether competent at their own emotional expression. They may or may not have known any better or done any better than we're doing now. They didn't receive formal instruction either. Their behaviors were passed down from their parents, and their parents' parents. We pick up genealogical or generational baggage in the form of behavior patterns and beliefs. When we wake up and begin to become more aware, we have the opportunity to change the way we handle our emotions and behaviors in the moment. First, we have to become aware of those emotions and behaviors before expecting to change them. Then, we can make a powerful leap forward.

We're not going to beat ourselves up for things we've done in the past, because we can see we were doing the best that we knew how at that time. We weren't necessarily taught productive strategies, or given specific instructions, but we can learn them now. Now that we're more aware of our past tendencies, we know we can change how we show up in our lives and the world.

As we investigate new ways to deal with our emotions, you will remember that our emotions are derived from our needs (Chapter Three). Whether you're aware of it consciously or not, everything you do is because you want something. Think about that for a minute. Everything you do is because you have a need that you want to see fulfilled or met. Every decision you make is based on your desire to *be*, *do*, or *have* something that will lead to happiness, joy, fulfillment, inspiration, passion, and contentment.

Self-Reflection:
Recognizing Old Strategies
and Creating New Ones

- *Take some time to think about how your emotions are derived from your needs. When your needs are met, you respond happily. When your needs are not met, they generate emotional discomfort, physical restlessness, and mental uncertainty.*

- *Next, think of something you did today—it needn't be anything particularly monumental—a conversation you had, an errand you ran, or a simple choice you made.*

- *Consider for a few moments why you did whatever it was you did. What drove your action, your behavior, or your choice in that moment? Write down whatever comes up.*

- *Now, think of a decision you made recently—something of slightly (or largely) more importance than an everyday lifestyle choice.*

- *Again, take some time to recall why you made the decision that you did. What drove your behavior, or what was the reason for making the decision you made? What was your intended outcome or purpose for doing what you did? Write down whatever comes up.*

- *You are likely seeing a pattern in your notes that illustrates how the choices and decisions you make, both large and small, are all for a specific reason—even if you weren't consciously aware of the reasons in the moment you took action.*

- *If at any point your revelations point to your having done something for someone else, or even for the greater good of humanity—if you keep asking the question "For what purpose did I do this? What am I getting in return?" you will eventually bring out your own personal reason for it.*

- *Remember that every decision you make is based on your desire to be, do, or have something that will lead to greater happiness, joy, fulfillment, inspiration, passion, purpose, and contentment.*

Changing Your Interpretation

Every experience we have results in feelings of comfort or discomfort. In Tom Robbins' book *Still Life with Woodpecker*, he writes, "There are only two mantras, yum and yuck. Mine is yum." He says that you can always listen to your body when you're making a choice or decision. If your body responds with a yummy feeling, then you move forward. If your body responds with tension, constriction, and anxiety, you don't make the choice to move forward.

Every experience we have either lends to a feeling of comfort or discomfort, and this is how we gauge whether we want to repeat, or not repeat, the same or similar experiences. Emotions are the energetic perception of what is occurring in or around us. They're derived from our needs. If something brings you a sense of happiness, comfort, or good feelings, chances are you're going to pursue it. Whereas if something generates discomfort or feels yucky, you're likely to move away from it as quickly as possible.

One of the four principles for transformation in Chapter Two is "Perception is Interpretation." How you perceive and interpret your experiences will color your thoughts, words, actions, and behaviors, which will in turn determine the choices you make in any given situation.

For example, if someone challenges your belief system by sharing their own views about politics, religion, or family, you might become defensive, lashing out with your words or actions. In your need to defend your own beliefs or point of view, you might show up as being righteous or indignant in your position, committed to convincing the other person that they're wrong and your point of view is right. Holding our position and defending our point of view is a fairly common response.

But what if you had a different interpretation of the same scenario? Let's say someone challenges your belief system, and instead of interpreting it as "They're wrong and I'm right," you simply notice that people have different opinions. You honor and respect that people see things differently; they have contrasting opinions and distinctive preferences based on how they are perceiving and interpreting the world in which we live. Rather than feeling defensive, you feel curious about their viewpoint. If you look around, you might notice that some of the people you most respect and trust have this kind of response to what other people would see as a conflict. Which response seems more productive?

Another example: Say your partner left your relationship out of the blue and blindsided you. It's not uncommon to feel distressed, heartbroken, or full of anxiety, like you're spinning out of control. Perhaps you find yourself unable to function normally on a daily basis. You wake up feeling depressed and hopeless, your days drag on forever, and all you can think about is how empty your life is now that this person is gone. Maybe you even find yourself doing irrational things like texting your ex's phone to see if you can "talk," or going to the places where they hang out in hopes of reconnecting with them. The way you are perceiving what happened and how you are interpreting what it means will determine how you respond.

Let's consider another way to interpret this situation. Maybe shift your perception and view it as an opportunity to remove yourself from a situation that wasn't a long-term fit. You remind yourself you'd never want to be in a relationship with someone who doesn't want to be in a relationship with you. What if you could just feel grateful for the time you had together? What if you could wish the other person well, send them off with love, then take some time to work through your sadness and disappointment? This calm, cool, and collected response to not having your emotional needs met in this situation might seem unrealistic, but trust me: Responding this way to a breakup unfolds much more potential for learning and growth. Ultimately, it frees up your energy to prepare you for the relationship you're meant to be in. Which approach would make you happier in the long and short run?

Let's take the example of your company announcing that it is downsizing. For many people, that stirs up fear and anxiety about job security. In their effort to gain the boss' favor and keep their position, they start working longer hours, coming into the office earlier and staying later. They'll send emails at midnight, work on weekends, and take on more projects than they can possibly handle, all to prove themselves as a valuable asset.

But what if you chose a different interpretation? "Okay, the company needs to tighten things up. This is an opportunity for me to either step up or step away. What do I really I want to be doing in my line of work? Is this job a good fit for me? Am I inspired when I go to work? Do I love what I do each day?" If the answer is yes, then you might ask yourself, "Where do I need to step up, or in what ways could I be contributing differently?" You may end up working a little harder, but you're doing it from a place of confidence, not fear and insecurity. Your coworkers might be freaking out while you have chosen a different interpretation and are seeing the situation in a completely different light.

An awareness of the principle for transformation of perception and interpretation enables you to look at what's happening through a different lens, so you can become a conscious and empowered co-creator of your life. You don't have to enact old behavior patterns anymore. It's not about being a phony or a Pollyanna (though I think she had the right idea). It's about choosing a perspective that serves you and supports what you want out of life.

In live trainings and with my clients, I often ask, "What is it that determines whether you interpret something as good or bad? Right or wrong? Scary or safe? Comfortable or uncomfortable?" The response is pretty much always, "My past experiences are what determine how I interpret something." And that is almost correct. It's actually your *perception and interpretation* of the experience that determine how you interpret it.

This is why it's important to acknowledge that your perception is, in fact, directing your interpretation. In every given moment of every day, how you see something is *not* the only reality. There are multiple realities, and it's up to you to choose whether you will be a victim of circumstances or intentionally elect to go down the path of the empowered individual. Now that you know you have a choice as to how you view circumstances, events, and people, you can choose a point of view that doesn't trigger negative emotional reactivity and create new baggage.

Self-Reflection:
Consciously Choosing How You Want
Interpret Your Experiences

- *Make a list of current challenges you may be having in your life: an argument with your spouse, a medical diagnosis, someone else's medical diagnosis, a conflicting opinion or viewpoint with your boss or a family member. It can be anything that you are currently viewing as a problem, obstacle, or challenge.*

- *Make some notes about this problem, anyone else involved, and how you are currently viewing it. Are you looking at what's right about the situation and viewing it positively, or are you looking at it from the viewpoint that it's wrong, bad, or unfair? Are you blaming another person for how things have turned out?*

- *Become aware of what it's costing you to stay focused on all that is seemingly wrong with this situation. Write down anything that comes to mind. What do you need to let go of or accept?*

- *Next take some time to shift into a place of observing your problem objectively. Remove yourself from being the subject of your experience to seeing yourself and whatever is playing out more from a distance. Imagine that you are observing what is happening, rather than being the one experiencing it.*

- *From this new vantage point, allow yourself to see any positive lessons or gifts that have come about as a result of this challenge you are experiencing. Focus on what could be interpreted as being right or necessary for your own growth and transformation. How can you turn this challenge into an opportunity to learn something new, heal an aspect of yourself, or find the wisdom buried beneath the surface?*

- *Notice how much better you feel as a result of being able to consciously choose how you would like to interpret life's obstacles and challenges.*

Taking Responsibility

Another principle for transformation from Chapter Two is responsibility. Emotionally intelligent people take responsibility for how they choose to show up and how they opt to perceive and interpret their experiences. They take responsibility for their actions and are accountable for following through with what they need to do to live the life they want. People who take responsibility for how their lives are unfolding have become skilled in extracting the life lessons from their experiences, and they learn how to make more conscious choices moving forward. When you act with emotional intelligence and become fluent in being responsible, you lighten your load tenfold.

Break Old Patterns, Create Positive Habits

We all operate on cyclical patterns of action, memory, and desire. Action, memory, desire—it's like a karmic hamster wheel of life. At some point, we took an action. That action created a memory that generated a desire to either repeat—or not repeat—the pattern.

I used to be "highly motivated" by Starbucks, which is my funny way of saying I was hooked! Each morning on the way to work, I'd stop for my venti vanilla latté. Every afternoon around three or four o'clock, I would venture out for my second (or third) Starbucks. This action generated memories of the previous times I'd had a vanilla latté. It felt so warm in my hands; it was so sweet and creamy and comforting. When I drank that vanilla latté, I immediately felt comforted. I also noticed it gave me a little bit of a jolt as the caffeine kicked in. I really liked that. It gave me my second wind in the later part of the day. I felt like I was back in my zone!

Each vanilla latté experience created a memory of that comfort and surge of energy to help me get through the rest of my day.

It sure seemed like a win-win. The memory led to my desire to repeat that very same action every single day. It became my pattern, my routine. If the memory is perceived as being a positive one, the desire will influence us to make the same decision again. If the memory of the experience didn't feel good, our desire will be to not repeat that same action. When conscious choice-making leads to a new and different action, this is called a "pattern interrupt." This is where we can put an end to non-serving cycles.

As a technique, a pattern interrupt is a way of changing your mental, emotional, or behavioral state or strategy. Learning how to create a pattern interrupt can help you install new behaviors that in turn will get you out of old, unwanted cycles.

To end a cycle, you must first become aware that you're caught up in one. If you feel like you're on a merry-go-round, and you're just spinning, spinning, spinning, you've gotten yourself into a cyclical pattern. The longer you spin, the dizzier you get. You've entered a trance-like state of existence and are just going through the motions, not paying attention to much of anything, let alone your choices or actions. You're on auto-pilot and doing the same things over and over again, without being a conscious co-creator of your life. This can happen with healthy, productive cycles just as easily as it can with unhealthy patterns. Eventually, if you become aware that you're stuck in a negative cycle, you can jump off that merry-go-round. By stepping out of the cycle, you can look back to observe, "Wow, this is a repetitive pattern that's just not working."

The moment you become aware of the cycle, you can create a pattern interrupt. When we find ourselves stuck in these ruts of life, the first key is to become aware of them. You can't change something if you're not consciously aware that it's happening. So, the first step is to become aware that you are repeating an unhealthy pattern and to identify that pattern.

The second step is to closely observe yourself while you're running the pattern so you can pinpoint the precise moment where you step into it. That critical moment is where you need to install a new behavior. Finally, you need to practice your new pattern diligently and repeatedly until it becomes a new habit.

Many of us, however, recognize our patterns and choose to ignore them. We tell ourselves it's not that bad, and we go on about our lives as if the problem doesn't exist. Those distractions that help you avoid difficult feelings work much in the same way as the *action-memory-desire* patterns. We distract ourselves by taking an action to avoid whatever it is we know we need to deal with. The memory we create is, "That made me feel good and it got my mind off my problems for a while." The memory of feeling better after avoiding dealing with the issues leads to the desire to repeat that same distraction the next time we feel discomfort. "Last time, I had a glass of wine and I felt better." But the distraction never resolves the issue. It just puts it on the back burner for a while until something new happens and the water begins to boil over again. This is how we create new baggage—through avoidance.

Self-Reflection:
Creating a Pattern Interrupt

- *Identify an unhealthy pattern you are running in your own life. This should be fairly simple to spot, because it's the same thing you're doing over and over again.*

- *Where does it derail you? Is it in your relationship? At work? Is it derailing your overall health? Your ability to set and enforce boundaries?*

- *What's it costing you to keep doing it? Is it costing you time, money, the ability to sleep soundly through the night, your sense of self-worth?*

- *What would be possible for you if you stopped it and created a new, positive, healthy pattern?*

- *What is a new action or behavior—something that is different from the way you used to do things—you could do that will reinforce your decision to interrupt the old pattern and replace it with something new?*

- *Do it! This means you need to keep doing it over and over again until it becomes a habit. Here is where consistency and repetition are necessary for you to create the change you are seeking. You'll know you've successfully installed a new habit when your old pattern is no longer present.*

Dealing with Difficult Emotions in the Now

The techniques above help with lesser issues. But what about those strong overwhelming emotions that pop up during the day and follow us home? How do we deal with significant emotions as they come up in our daily lives so they don't turn into baggage? Learning how to navigate our experiences in the moment is a very similar process to that of digging up previously stored baggage. First and foremost, it's about: 1) being present in the moment and looking closely at what just happened, 2) noticing how we feel in the moment, 3) identifying what it is we need in this moment, and 4) determining how to move forward consciously so we unfold the highest level of potential for ourselves and everyone else involved.

First, go to a place that is comfortable and where you will not be disturbed. Minimize distractions by turning your phone off, putting the pets outside the room, and letting your family know you're going to be taking some time to do some self-reflection. Have your journal and a pen ready. Prepare yourself and your space in any way you feel will best support your process. Take a deep breath and remind yourself why you are doing this work. It may help to remind yourself of the commitments in Chapter Two.

Briefly, these commitments are to:

1. Be fully present in this process and your life. This means to do the exercises outlined in this book and take them with you out into your day-to-day interactions. Notice how you react to people who trigger you and situations that don't unfold as you would like them to. Practice the techniques you're learning here and try them in your daily life.

2. Focus on responding, not reacting. Take responsibility for your thoughts, words, and actions. Recognize that you—and only you—have the ability to change the way you think, speak, and behave.

3. Be authentic with yourself and others. Refrain from hiding behind your reasons and excuses and, instead, be honest in your assessment of how you are handling your emotions and navigating your relationships. Be honest with others, and speak your truth from your heart.

4. Express yourself. Speak your truth to yourself and others, whether by journaling or speaking up—whatever keeps you from holding things inside.

5. Abandon your comfort zone. Stretch yourself physically and psychologically, and open your mind and heart as in bodhichitta.

6. Honor silence as best you can throughout your process. Being in silence connects you more deeply to who you are at the core of your being. Silence helps you to get clear and honest with yourself. It enables you to hear the voice of intuition and higher guidance.

7. Last, but not least, come back to the commitment of becoming your best self.

Now that you've recommitted, the second step is to settle into present moment awareness. That simply means to bring your mind to the here and the now. Begin by closing your eyes and taking some deep breaths. Let the worries and busyness of your day melt away. Come into the present moment, right here, right now.

As you settle into present moment awareness, acknowledge that your emotional states are driving your choices in every moment. Recognize how you currently deal with stress and emotional upset, and once again make a conscious choice to change those old patterns and behaviors.

Using the Five Questions for Navigating the Now

Now that you've revisited your commitments and settled into the present moment, you're ready to lean into compassionate self-inquiry. This is a similar process to the one we used for digging up our baggage in the previous chapters, with slight variations. The first question is, "What just happened?" Remember to simply observe without any judgment—without evaluating the people involved, sticking with the facts only. Do some journaling about this.

The next question is, "How are you feeling in this moment?" What emotions do you feel? Get specific: Is it anger? Sadness? Fear? Shame? Jealousy? Resentment? Guilt? Lean into the emotion as it arises. Where do you feel it in your body? Breathe into it. Allow the energy to move through you. Make some notes in your journal about the emotions that are arising within you and how you are experiencing them.

The third step is to ask, "What do I need in this situation that I'm not receiving? What boundary has been crossed or violated?" Get to the bottom of what just happened in that moment, how it's making you feel, what it was that you needed, and how that need was not met. Remember that our emotions are derived from our needs, and chances are, whatever just happened in some way prevented you from getting what you needed in the moment. Identify what that was or is, and then take some time to jot down some notes in your journal.

The fourth question is to ask yourself, "What do I get out of holding on to what happened and how I am currently feeling?" Look for any secondary gain here. Ask yourself, honestly, "What will I get or what will happen if I hold on to this emotional pain?" On the flip side, ask yourself, "What would be possible if I choose to perceive and interpret my experiences differently, to turn this into a powerful learning opportunity?" Journal what comes up for you as you explore the questions on each side of this equation. What will happen if you hold on, and what is possible if you let it go?

Finally, ask yourself, "How would I like to consciously respond to this situation?" Ask yourself what action you need to take in this moment to consciously and lovingly move through this. Write down any action steps that you know you need to take. These steps could entail a practice of some kind, or setting up a support structure, having a conversation with someone, upholding your own boundaries—anything that will help you to move through this challenging situation in a very conscious, focused, and heart-centered way.

Self-Reflection:
Navigating the Now

- *Take some time to settle into the present moment.*

- *Find a comfortable seat, close your eyes, and begin to focus on the inhalation and exhalation of your breath. Use your breath to become aware of any thoughts, images, physical sensations, or feelings.*

- *Without making any judgments, observe what just happened and take a few minutes to make some notes—write down only the facts, as opposed to your thoughts, judgments, or assumptions.*

- *Now, get in touch with how you are feeling emotionally. Silently and with self-compassion, allow yourself to connect with your emotions. How are you feeling inside? Identify the emotion(s) you're experiencing right now, in this moment. Make some notes in your journal.*

- *Next, ask yourself what it was you needed at the time of the event that you didn't receive. Was there a boundary of some sort that was violated? Did you need to feel valued or respected? Loved or cherished? Included or worthy? Bring yourself to a place of understanding what need went unmet.*

- *See now if you can pinpoint what you could gain from holding on to any negative emotions or limiting beliefs that arose as a result of what happened. Is there secondary gain—a reason that you think serves you, but in actuality prevents you from moving powerfully forward in this moment?*

- *Last, ask yourself how you would like to proceed. What action do you need to take in this moment that would diffuse the situation—for yourself and/or others—and allow you to move into a place of acceptance as you redirect your energy toward a more positive outcome.*

Own and Release the Emotion

During compassionate self-inquiry, you ask powerful questions and collect the information that arises. Next, you must take responsibility for what you're feeling without projecting it out into the world or others. Own what you're feeling as being yours. It's your emotion; it's your belief; it's your stuff. It's not somebody else's, and nobody put it on you. This emotion you're feeling was already inside you, a part of you. That person, circumstance, or experience that happened to stir it up is a gift in disguise (although it probably doesn't seem that way in the moment) and is providing you with an incredible opportunity to learn and/or reconcile unresolved emotional baggage. How do you know if it's an emotion elicited by a current event or old baggage accumulated from past events? The best test is whether the emotion is warranted and an appropriate response to the current situation. Being slightly ticked at being interrupted might be warranted (current emotion). Becoming furious at being interrupted probably isn't (old baggage). Feeling very sad that someone you love has died is appropriate and natural (current emotion). Falling apart every time someone even mentions death really isn't (old baggage).

Once you've owned it, express the emotion to yourself in private in whatever way you prefer. Many people spend time journaling about their responses to the questions above. Some people like to express through art, such as writing, music, painting, drawing, or through poetry. Others express through some type of movement like dancing or martial arts. You may want to be vocal, talking it through with yourself or even shouting.

If you're feeling particularly ramped up, go into a private place where you won't disturb or upset others. Go into a room or out into nature and just scream, shout, swear, and throw your arms around. If you need more release, grab a baseball bat and beat on a pillow. Do whatever you need to do to express the emotion you're feeling. Remember, emotions are energy in motion, and it's important to continue to mobilize the energy so it can move through you—and release.

You can also choose to personify the emotion. Ask, "What is the emotion?" Give it a label, like anger or hurt. "What or whom does this emotion represent? Notice if this emotion fits into other themes and patterns that you previously identified.

Then, ask yourself (or the personified emotion), "What is the lesson I need to see, or the message I need to hear? What do I need to know or understand to shift how I am perceiving this circumstance? What is the wisdom or lesson available to me right now?"

Next, integrate the personified emotion through loving acknowledgement and conversation. Commit to some action within the next twenty-four hours that declares you're integrating this aspect of yourself. Choose to move powerfully forward in a positive way, and use what you've learned to grow and evolve as a human being. Journal about your experience and the conversation you had with your personified emotion.

Handling Emotions in the Midst of "Battle"

The previous approach is good to apply when you are dealing with something challenging that's happening in your life, but you aren't standing face to face with it in the moment. It's a good practice when you're at home, you've created the space to unpack what is happening, and you have the time to really dig into a process. But let's say you're not all cozy in your special space with a hot cup of tea. Let's say you're standing in the office and your boss is screaming at you. Or you're sitting in a restaurant and your significant other is breaking up with you. Or you're in the doctor's office and you get news about your health that isn't positive. In that moment, you aren't in the space for, nor do you have time to, journal using compassionate self-inquiry to figure out what wisdom you're gaining or what your most positive next move should be. Right then, in that moment, you're caught up in your emotions. All you want to do is rage it out or run and hide.

If someone's ranting at you or somehow hurting or threatening you, chances are that you'll start to check out, at least to some extent, while you process what is happening. Next, your internal dialogue revs up: "What the hell's wrong with this person?" or "Oh my God. Is this actually happening?" We're swept away from present moment awareness and are immediately slammed into the fight-or-flight response. This is where we get into our own thought process of perceiving, interpreting, evaluating, and labeling, which in turn revs up our emotions.

One of my greatest mentors and dear friend, Deepak Chopra, teaches the STOP acronym. This is a simple and highly effective tool for creating a pattern interrupt—snapping you out of the situation and back into the present moment. "S" stands for stop. Stop engaging, stop what you're doing.

"T" stands for take a deep breath. Taking a deep breath might mean walking around the block, going into a different room, or taking five deep breaths while you're standing there. If you have the option, it might mean to sleep on it and come back to the situation later. If you can, create some distance, a buffer space. If you can't, just take a deep breath to help your physiology relax from its fight-or-flight reaction and do your best to go into peripheral vision—which I explain immediately following the STOP acronym.

"O" stands for observe. Observe what's happening—internally and externally—and choose to be present from the place of observation and witnessing. Rather than internalizing what's happening, taking what's being said personally or making it about yourself, shift into observer mode. It's similar to the first question we use in the process we did earlier in this chapter: "What just happened?" Observe without evaluation.

"P" stands for proceed. After simply observing the situation for a moment, ask yourself, "How would I like to respond to this? What kind of person do I want to be in this scenario?" Remember, how you proceed is always a choice. You can proceed by fight-or-flight: throwing your hands around, pushing and shoving, or running away. You can act out the psychological equivalents of these, lashing out verbally or withdrawing and going silent. Observe first, then ask how you want to proceed and remind yourself that you have a choice.

Going into peripheral vision, also known in the Hawaiian language as *hakalau*, is a quick and highly effective tool for helping to reduce the negative charge when the heat of the moment is a little too hot to handle.

The process is simple: When you are feeling highly charged in the moment, pick a spot on the wall to focus on that is just above eye level. It can be anything: a pattern in the paint, the way the light casts a shadow on the wall, where the two corners of a windowsill meet. In the yogic tradition, we call this a *Drishti*, or point of focus. As you focus on it, begin now to pay attention to the peripheral part of your vision without looking away from the point of focus. Notice how the emotional charge begins to soften, or it may diminish entirely. This is a good practice to do whenever you're feeling like you're not in control of your emotions in the moment or if you just need to refocus and get centered before taking action. By doing this, you increase the likelihood that you will respond from a place of conscious awareness rather than reacting like a lunatic.

This art of navigating your emotions in the now is something that takes practice, and it's not going to turn out perfectly every single time. There will be instances when you don't catch yourself in time and you react in a way that you're not proud of, or that you later regret. That's okay—you're human.

155

I've been working with this for about a decade and, for the most part, I can think pretty quickly on my feet in the midst of a dramatic or unsettling interaction. I'm usually able to formulate my response in the moment. Yet, I'm not perfect. There are still times when I realize I could have handled an issue better. Here's the point: The more you work with the five questions for "navigating the now," the more adept you become at responding in empowering ways in the moment. Practice the STOP acronym. It'll stop you in your tracks from acting out old behaviors and patterns that no longer serve you. Practice *Hakalau*, using a focal point and going into peripheral vision to reduce the charge when things are lit up. In time, you will begin to master working with your emotions rather than being ruled by them.

Navigating your emotions in the moment is not an exact science. There are tools and techniques you'll benefit from immediately and that you'll love practicing. You can swap out a certain tool because it's not the right tool for you, or if it's not right at the time for what you are dealing with. Whatever tools and techniques you have in your toolbox, be willing to explore and experiment with what works best for you in that moment and for that experience.

Be flexible, be patient, and allow yourself to be human. Take the time you need to grieve and process your emotions in the moment, without trying to rush yourself through the process to the other end. In western society, we're so accustomed to taking a quick pill or going after a quick fix. But when it comes to navigating emotions, moving through the process and allowing ourselves whatever time we need will truly benefit us in the long term.

8

Your Emotional Support System

"Where there is negative thinking, let there be reflection to the contrary."

- Patanjali, circa. 600 A.D.

In this chapter, we'll talk about building an emotional support system to sustain the progress you've made thus far. Everything you've been doing up to this point has been specifically designed to help you become aware of the automatic habits and patterns that don't serve you and others that do serve you. For things to change, you've got to change. For things to get better in your life, you're the one who needs to get better. It's time to look at your habits and investigate the patterns in your life even more deeply. Do they serve you in becoming the person you wish to be? Do they support your emotional integrity and health? If they do not serve you, what new habits and patterns could you create?

A behavior turns into a habit by constant repetition until it becomes automatic. The compounded effect of little habits repeated over time will either work for or against you. One of my favorite books of all time is *The Slight Edge* by Jeff Olson. Olson talks about the importance of doing little, positive things every single day. He says that over time, this is what will make the biggest difference in your life. Daily practices are what create habits.

We've worked to identify and release past negative emotions, unconscious decisions, and limiting beliefs. We've worked through the process of forgiveness. We're now aware of better ways to navigate our emotional upsets as they occur. Next, we want to instill habits to support the gains we've made. Your habits come from your daily activities. Your activities are the result of the choices you make in each moment, and your choices come from your habits of thought. The key is to continue making choices that empower us.

Throughout your process of self-inquiry and witnessing, of identifying and of letting go, you've created a newer, more empowered version of yourself that is now emotionally integrated and freer. We call this *moksha*, which is a Sanskrit word that means emotional liberation.

Self-Reflection:
Taking Stock

Take a few moments to reflect on all the work you have done up to this point. Identify if anything might be left that needs to be resolved. Ask yourself:

- *Is there an area of my life where I can visualize moving from constriction to total and complete expansion?*

- *If so, what does my life look like in that totally free, happy and expanded state? What does it feel like after I've consciously chosen to let go of that constriction, that thing that no longer serves me?*

- *Is there anything I'm still holding on to that's no longer serving me?*

- *If so, what can I do to release my grip and experience more freedom and choice?*

Mindfulness

To support your emotional well-being, train yourself in the art of mindfulness—paying special attention to your thoughts, words, and actions. Everything we think, say, and do is planting a seed for its reciprocal energy to return to us. Your heart is always listening to your thoughts, observing your words, and responding to your behaviors. That which you go looking for, you are sure to find. If we assume we'll be hurt, we'll find someone or something to hurt us. If we assume that we will fail, we'll find ways to fail. On the flip side, if we assume that the universe is working in our favor, we'll find all kinds of opportunities popping up. It's a self-fulfilling prophecy. We project our prior experiences—and the conclusions we drew from those experiences—onto the present moment. The way we consistently think about our lives is what determines how our future will unfold. What we focus on is what we produce.

It's important to be mindful of your thoughts, what you say, and how you act. Are your words, thoughts, and actions supporting your vision of your best self? Or are you focusing on the past and what you *don't* want?

Self-Reflection:
Becoming Mindful of Your Thoughts,
Words, and Actions

As part of your daily mindfulness practice, spend time observing your thoughts, words (spoken and written), and actions (or inaction).

Take 15-30 minutes in your day to silently observe how you are perceiving, interpreting, and interacting with yourself, others, and the world you live in. Listen to your thoughts; see images floating through your mind; notice the words that flow from your mouth and hands; observe the ways in which you react.

- *Your thoughts: Do they amplify a positive energetic vibration, or do they ripple out negativity?*
- *Your words: Are they true? Are they necessary? Are they kind? If you answer no to any of these questions, consider the repercussions of your words before expressing them.*
- *Your actions: Are they moving you powerfully forward in your life, or are they keeping you stuck in the past? Will they have a positive influence on others and the blueprint you leave behind in this world?*

As your awareness increases, you will find yourself doing this process automatically as you move through your day. At the beginning, and while you are establishing this practice, it's best to schedule time in your day to consciously place your awareness on it.

Recapitulation

Recapitulation is a process of reviewing your day each night before you go to bed. You simply recall the day quickly, noticing how you felt about each encounter. You might notice something that nags at you or didn't feel good. What about that didn't feel good? It's a contemplative process of, "I knew I felt off when I did that. When I said that, it didn't feel good. Why didn't it feel good? What could I have done better?" It's not about beating yourself up. It's becoming conscious of the lessons from your day and using them to create a more positive tomorrow.

Self-Reflection:
Recapitulating Your Day

- *Each evening before you go to sleep, sit upright in your bed and close your eyes.*
- *Deepen your breath and place your awareness on the inhalation and exhalation as you settle comfortably into the present moment.*
- *Play back your day on the screen of your awareness.*
- *Begin from the moment when you woke up and move through each of your experiences, conversations, thoughts, and behaviors all the way up to this moment.*
- *Play back your day relatively quickly—as though you're watching a movie reel—not spending too much time on the details. This shouldn't take more than one to two minutes.*
- *Just observe what you see and take note of anything that stands out. You may notice that you felt good about how you flowed through your day, or perhaps you observe where you could have handled something differently. The purpose is to simply observe where you did well and where you can make improvements the next day.*
- *When you have finished, turn out the lights, settle into your bed, and sleep well.*

Reframing

A simple yet powerful practice to support you is reframing, or turning challenges into opportunities. As I've become more aware of the importance of reframing, whenever I have the thought "I have a problem," or "There's a problem," or "This is a challenge," I immediately reframe it to, "Okay. I have an interesting opportunity here." Just as you did in previous chapters, whenever you encounter challenging people, obstacles, or unexpected twists and turns in your day, look for the opportunity. Turn it into an exciting learning experience rather than a burden or an obstacle. It may not *feel* exciting in the moment, but you get my drift.

Reframing is basically asking yourself, "How can I see this differently and in a positive light?" Remember that for every person who freaks out during a rainstorm, someone else loves it. That traffic jam? Gives you time to chill out and regroup before getting home from the office. Not chosen for a job you wanted? Something better is waiting for you. Break up with a boyfriend? Hey, you don't have to shave your legs for a while. Reframing is when you decide to turn lemons into lemonade. It's the perspective you choose to take because it supports who you are becoming.

When you reframe something, you are telling your unconscious mind to process the event in a different way. Keep in mind that your unconscious doesn't process negatives directly, so make sure your reframe is in positive terms. Rather than saying, "I am not stressed about this traffic jam," it is more effective to say, "I appreciate this traffic jam for the extra time it gives me to relax and enjoy some good tunes."

Self-Reflection:
Reframing

Whenever you experience a negative thought or have a less-than-desirable event, take a moment to practice the STOP exercise. Remember: S = stop, T = take a deep breath or a walk, O = observe what's happening, and P = proceed consciously.

As you are in the O = observation step, bring to mind the issue at hand, anyone else involved, and how you are currently viewing it. Chances are, you're looking at it from a negative perspective, which only serves to perpetuate more negative feelings and viewpoints. This, in turn, adversely affects your physiology and can have a detrimental effect on your overall health and well-being.

Rather than focusing on the negative aspect of what is occurring, allow yourself to see any positive messages or lessons that are available to you right now.

Make a conscious choice to view what is happening through a different lens or with a positive light. Sometimes it helps to remind yourself that everything happens for a reason, even if we're not able to understand that in the moment. Ask yourself, "What is a possible positive reason for this to be happening?"

Notice how the situation shifts when you go from an extreme negative viewpoint to recognizing that there is a message, lesson, or gift in everything that happens. It's up to us to find the gold beneath the rubble.

Meeting Our Needs from Within

In Chapter Three, I discussed that our emotions are derived from our needs being met or not being met. Most of us have been taught to fulfill those needs—attention, affection, appreciation, and acceptance—from outside of ourselves. We've been taught that happiness comes from something on the outside. We're taught to identify our happiness by our accomplishments, positions, and possessions.

From a very young age, we're told, "If you want to be happy, you need to go to college." Or, "If you want to be happy, you need to get into a great relationship." "If you want to be successful, you need to get a great education." "If you want to be accepted, you need to conform to society's rules or ideals about how you're supposed to show up in life." We're taught that we have to go out and seek something outside of ourselves. Few of us are taught to look *inside* ourselves for the attention, affection, appreciation, and acceptance we need.

Most of us start behaving in ways that we believe will lead to having our needs met from the outside. As a little kid, if we're told, "Don't say things like that," or "Don't behave that way in public," we learn to *not* express who we are, but to conform to get our needs met. "Oh, I can't show up in this particular way with this person if I want to feel accepted or appreciated, or get attention or receive affection." Of course, many of these learnings are a result of the efforts on our parents' part to teach us how to be good-natured, well-mannered people. The point I'm making is that, along the way, we also learn to hide aspects of who we are because of our need to please our caregivers and be acknowledged.

We learn from a very young age to wear different hats, and to build our personas, which are our public masks. We learn to show up in different ways, to carefully tailor our behavior to accommodate different people and different scenarios. Then, as we grow up, we wear different hats at school or when we're hanging out with different groups of friends. We show up differently in the workplace than we do in social settings, and differently than when we're at home.

As we move through life, we're constantly seeking appreciation, attention, affection, and acceptance from outside of ourselves in one form or another. And it works, to a certain extent. We can get a certain amount of satisfaction from buying new things. Retail therapy is always a great fix—for a few hours. We love a good shopping spree or buying a new car or a new toy, or whatever we think makes us feel better. And it does— for a while. But that feeling of being satiated doesn't last long.

At a certain point in our lives, we start to figure out that belongings, accomplishments, and things we acquire throughout life are incapable of satisfying our longing for true happiness. Even if we derive some temporary pleasure from these things, the feeling fades over time, causing us to experience a proportionate amount of disappointment.

We bought into the notion that if we want to be happy we should go to this school and get a certain type of job, drive a certain type of car, run in certain social circles, marry the right person, have a home in the right neighborhood, and do all these things in the right way. So, we tried to follow that plan. This is called *object referral.* Object referral is when we base our happiness, self-worth, or success on external factors: other people, successes in career, or material acquisitions.

But at the end of the day, we're left thinking, "What is missing and why am I not happy?" Our unmet needs can't be fulfilled by other people or material belongings, because as soon as those people or material things are gone, we are once again left feeling empty. We can only truly fill our four needs—attention, affection, appreciation, and acceptance—by ourselves within ourselves. This is called *self-referral*: looking within ourselves to find ways to meet our own needs, so we can learn how to be happy from the inside out. Once we learn how to live from this place, all the external things like adoration, acceptance, accomplishments, and things we acquire along the way are added bonuses. But they aren't the driving force behind whether or not we are truly happy.

Self-Reflection:
How You Meet Your Needs Now

Take out your journal and write down these four words: attention, affection, appreciation, and acceptance. Leave some space in-between, and take some time to think about the ways in which you go looking for each of these needs outside of yourself on a daily basis. How do you try to gain acceptance from other people to make you feel whole? What do you do to get attention? Write down whatever comes to you about these four needs.

First, identify the ways that you show up every day trying to get attention from the outside. Maybe you post on social media a lot to get attention, always checking how many "likes" you get. Maybe you dress in specific ways to get attention. Maybe you dominate a conversation or have to be the center of attention in a group. Maybe you're always the first to raise your hand in class, or maybe you're the class clown. Think about yourself in different situations. How do you try to get attention?

What are some of the ways you seek affection from outside yourself? Maybe you go around giving people hugs or center your conversations on how awful your current relationship is, hoping someone will console you. Maybe you seek inappropriate intimacy, not because you're feeling connected, but because sex can feel close to affection. But one-night stands can't really fill that deep need for affection.

Follow the same process for appreciation. How do you seek appreciation? A common example is, "I come into work early and I'm the last one to leave. I send emails late at night so my boss will see that I'm working and consider me for a raise or a promotion, or my teammates will think, 'Oh my, she takes care of everything. She's so amazing.'" Maybe you overextend yourself or try to please everyone to your own detriment.

Finally, consider how you try to get acceptance from others. Maybe you pretend to agree with everything your coworkers say whether you feel that way or not. Maybe you focus on activities your significant other loves while leaving your own interests behind. Maybe you attend a certain church or vote a certain way, or wear a certain hairstyle or clothing label, all in the attempt to fit in and be accepted by others.

The point is not to make you feel bad about yourself for the ways in which you seek these things, but rather to bring awareness to your behavior patterns so you can create a pattern interrupt and change them. Everything begins with awareness. If you don't have an awareness of how you go about your behaviors, how can you expect to change them? So, first, you have to be aware of how you deal with your needs. This can be an incredibly eye-opening process if you allow yourself to dig deep and be totally honest with yourself. Now, let's flip this and look at the other side of the coin.

Happiness needs to be created from the inside out. We stop looking at everyone and everything around us to make us feel whole and happy. We start looking at how we can create this for ourselves.

Here's the caveat: When you ask yourself, "How can I provide these things to myself?" think of things that do *not* involve other people, your pet, or spending money. It's easy to think, "Oh, I'll get my need for affection from my dog," or "I can show myself appreciation by buying a new pair of shoes or a new set of golf clubs," or "I'll give myself attention by attending a retreat or getting a spa treatment."

These things aren't bad, but the point is to figure out how we can do it in a way that doesn't involve someone or something else. What if you don't have the money to afford a new dress, retreat or massage? What if you live in a place where there are no golf courses? What if your beloved pet dies or you don't have one to begin with? What if you don't have a partner or spouse, or a parent or best friend? The point is, "How can I give myself attention, affection, appreciation, and acceptance so that I can learn to create my own true happiness?"

Self-Reflection:
Ways to Meet Your Needs from Within

The second part of this exercise is to write the same four words—attention, affection, appreciation, and acceptance—leaving some space after each one. Contemplate, "How can I provide this to myself?" and jot down whatever comes to you.

I get it. This is a different way of thinking, so it might take some brainstorming. For many people, the ways you seek to fulfill your needs from *outside* yourself are probably easier to list, and the list is longer. It's easy to identify all the ways in which we expect other people to meet our needs. At first, the list of ways to get needs met from *within* might be pretty short. This is where I'd like to remind you that it's about quality, not quantity. It's also about becoming aware of how we currently operate so we can adjust our behaviors.

When I've taken people through this second part of the exercise, they often just sit there staring at me blankly. Sometimes, they even get grumpy with me. When I ask if there is a problem, the response usually sounds something like, "Why can't I use money?!" (even though I just explained why), or "I can only think of one or two things," or sometimes I hear a defeated voice reply with "I can't think of anything at all." And that is perfectly okay. We simply haven't been taught to meet our own needs. We've been taught since infancy to rely upon others to serve us. Think about when you were a baby. All you had to do was cry out and your mom was there, constantly trying to figure out, "Okay, does she need food? Does he need his diaper changed? Is she teething? Is he tired? Does she just need to be cuddled?" Since day one, for most of us, someone has been there to figure all this out and provide it to us.

So, naturally, it may take some creative thinking to figure out how to fill your own needs from the inside out. In my workshops, attendees have come up with ideas for attention like, "I can give myself attention by meditating every day, and being more present to how my body feels while I am eating." "I can give myself attention by listing the things in my life that I'm grateful for." "I can uphold my boundaries and actually take downtime when needed, giving myself attention—the same attention I've always given everybody else."

For giving themselves affection, they came up with ideas like self-massage, giving yourself a little foot rub or shoulder squeeze, or a scalp massage as you're getting ready for bed. Some people thought about positive self-talk, talking to themselves in the loving way they would talk to their children. (Notice that what you do to self-fulfill one of the four needs can overlap into satisfying another need.)

How can you show yourself appreciation? I've heard students say, "I'll keep a progress journal, so I can high-five myself when I achieve a goal or keep track of the things I've accomplished this week, month, or year." Another idea is positive self-reflection, where you acknowledge yourself at the end of each day for all you did: "I appreciate the fact that I held strong in that conversation and didn't allow someone to railroad my position. I stuck up for myself." You can also appreciate yourself for trying something new, even if your attempt was not all that successful.

What about acceptance? How can we accept ourselves in this moment for who we are and how we are, without validation, justification, and the approval of others? One idea for giving yourself acceptance is to make a list of all your strengths and all the difficulties you've overcome. You can also make a list of all your so-called weaknesses and failures. In the overall scheme of things, how critical are those weaknesses? Are some of those "weaknesses" simply the biology you were born with? Or were they a version of you that needed to have certain experiences so you could evolve into the amazing person you are today? Acknowledge that, even in your worst of times, you were doing the best you could—given who you were at that time. Everything you've learned along the way has made you a better person.

Some students have created special mantras to interrupt the harsh voice of their internal critic: "People who love me would never talk to me like that." "Thanks for your opinion, and I am doing great with the resources I've been given."

When we seek acceptance from others, we often do it by conforming. How about making a list of all the ways you are different from others? How does that difference make a contribution? What are your unique talents and special gifts? What is wonderful about your differences, uniqueness, and the gifts you have to share with the world?

Strengthening Your Emotional Body

I think we all know that when we feel open, loving, confident, and strong, we're much more powerful than when we feel defensive, frightened, worried or depressed—wouldn't you agree? And now we know that we can choose how we feel in any moment. But how can we elicit those more positive emotional states daily?

Gratitude: One simple practice is to spend time each day feeling gratitude. Spend time each day to really appreciate all you're grateful for in your life. At first, you might think of surface things like, "I'm so grateful that it's sunny, warm, and a gorgeous day outside," or "I'm so grateful for my new job or the fact that today was a good day." I invite you to go a little deeper and ask yourself, "*Why* do I feel gratitude for the thing I identified?" To take it to the next level, you can ponder the questions, "What is really important to me about living? What are the treasures in my life?" For example, you might say, "I'm grateful for my friends and family who have supported me," or "I'm grateful for my health," or "I'm grateful for my ability to choose who I become." Spend some time really thinking about and appreciating things that have a lot of meaning to you and *why* those things are so special.

Creating an Anchor: I teach workshops that include techniques from NLP (Neuro Linguistic Programming). NLP has a powerful yet simple tool to help you enter a state of emotional balance almost instantly with a technique called anchoring. An anchor helps you shift from an unwanted state (i.e. anger, panic, or anxiety) to a more empowered, resourceful state (like confidence and calm) in the moment. Wouldn't you like to have total control of your emotional state at any time? That would be powerful, wouldn't it? This is why I love to work with the NLP technique of anchoring.

You already have several unconscious anchors that are being activated almost all the time. Hearing a certain song may anchor you to the first time you were in love. When you walk in the door at home and smell your house, that may be an anchor for you to feel relaxed. The smell of freshly baked chocolate chip cookies might anchor you back to your childhood. In any of these instances, if you're in a sour mood upon walking in the door or hearing that old song, these anchors immediately shift the way you are feeling, don't they? Exactly. When you learn how to create your own anchors specific to how you want to feel, they become a powerful ally. Just try it for yourself and see what results you get.

Let's check out how to do it. First, the idea is to get this anchor in place *before* you need to use it. It's like having a seatbelt; though you rarely need to use it, you always wear it when you're driving. In emergency, it's immediately there.

1. First, choose a "trigger" that sets the anchor's energy in motion. A trigger can be a physical movement, touch, or even a word. You could cross your fingers, stroke your ear, or say "Philadelphia" to yourself. Just make sure that the movement, touch, or word is not something you use all the time.

2. Now, design the kind of state you want to feel when you're in the middle of a difficult situation. Many people choose a sense of calm and feeling in control. They might add mental clarity and open-mindedness. Write down words that describe how you'd like to feel instead of angry, panicky, or melancholy.

3. Now, recall a time that you've felt what your words describe. Say you've chosen calm and in control. Think back to a specific time when you felt that way. Keep thinking about and imagining that time until you actually feel calm and in control emotionally and physically. (If you can't recall a specific time when *you* felt that way, think of someone who expresses the qualities of calm and in control. Imagine being that person. How does calm and in control feel emotionally? Physically? Get as much of that sensation as you can.) Amplify that feeling.

4. Next, activate your trigger. As you feel calmer and more in control, "activate" your trigger (cross your fingers, stroke your ear, or say the word you've chosen). Stop applying your trigger as soon as you feel the feelings of calm and in control start to fade away.

5. Do steps #3 and #4 several times, using another specific time when you felt totally calm and in control (or imagine another person with those qualities). Let the feelings flow through your body and emotions. Activate your trigger. Release your trigger as the feelings fade. This is called stacking the anchor. You're using several instances where you've felt the state you're wanting to use as your anchor to intensify it.

6. After several repetitions, test your new anchor. Start by clearing your mind by thinking about something totally unrelated, like your grocery list. Next, think about a person or situation that typically brings up a negative emotion. As soon as you feel that negative emotion, activate your trigger. Pay close attention to what happens to your emotions and body. Your trigger will call on those more positive responses you have anchored (in this example, calm and in control). Notice how the old reactions are replaced.

Take the time to create an anchor for yourself, and practice with it during situations that are not highly upsetting. Maybe you're just feeling a little out of sorts or irritated by something. Use your trigger to call up a more positive, productive state. By practicing, you'll learn to naturally use your anchor when you run into highly-charged situations as well.

Practicing Emotional Intelligence

Emotional intelligence is the ability to recognize and manage your own emotions. It includes the ability to respond appropriately. It also includes the ability to identify emotions in others and to respond appropriately. Some people are naturals at emotional intelligence, but many of us are not. We need practice to become grounded in it. Use these tools every day. Remember, new habits only become automatic when they are repeated over and over again.

Notice and Release: Through mindfulness, notice what happens each day, and process it using one or more of the techniques you learned earlier on. Did something stir up uncomfortable emotions, and old baggage? Lean into those emotions and do a release technique. Did someone offend you in some way? Or did you hurt or offend someone else? Use the forgiveness process. Stay aware and conscious of the choices you make as you move through each moment of the day. Stay on top of doing your emotional work, carving out fifteen or thirty minutes a day, or whatever time you require, to do your release practices. The more you use them, the easier and faster these practices will become for you.

Kindness: Having a positive effect on others is another way to generate happiness, joy, and fulfillment. One of the fastest ways to make yourself happy is to make someone else happy. Simply notice for yourself how good it makes you feel when you do something nice for someone else. It doesn't have to be something huge. Opening the door for an elderly person, smiling at the cashier, paying for coffee for the person in line behind you, giving someone a compliment or gift, helping out a coworker with a project deadline. Notice how doing these random acts of kindness increases your own emotional state in a positive way.

Fun: Bring the element of fun into every day. I had a client who subscribed to a humor website. Every day, she gets a joke in her email. It's her way of remembering to stay lighthearted and laugh a little. Some people carve out a specific time in their day for fun and leisure. It's something that they're going to do each and every day, like taking a yoga class, joining friends for happy hour, taking a walk on the beach, sitting down with the family at the end of the day to watch a great movie, or reading a good book at bedtime. Personally, I like to spend time on the trails with my horse. Schedule some form of downtime that brings you pleasure.

Meditation: Meditation is, by far, the most valuable and fundamental aspect of your daily mindfulness practice. While there are various approaches to meditation, I highly recommend you find an approach that involves sitting in stillness and silence for a period of time and just allowing yourself to "be." In today's world of glorifying "busy-ness," very few people know how to unplug and give themselves the gift of connecting within.

In his book *Secrets of Meditation* (which I highly recommend), my dear friend and master of wisdom, davidji, writes, "Meditation is a practice that transforms your entire physiology over time. Life takes on a different hue...a deeper meaning...a more universal understanding that pervades every cell of your being. The present-moment awareness you experience in meditation begins to flow throughout each thought, each conversation, each keystroke, and each breath."

Anyone can meditate. A common misconception about meditation among beginners is that you have to be able to stop your thoughts. False. Meditation is not about stopping your thoughts. It's about accessing the stillness and the quietude that resides in the space between them. Using a mantra-based meditation practice is a great way to ease into the practice. *Mantra* is a Sanskrit word that translates to a *tool* or *vehicle*. Put simply, it gives your conscious mind something to do while the real "you" drifts away from mental activity, physical sensations, and noises in the environment.

While I practice a specific style of mantra-based meditation, there are two simple approaches I like to share when I am teaching beginners to meditate. One is the mantra *So Hum* (Sanskrit translation is *I Am*). As you follow your breath in, silently think the word *So*; as you follow your breath out, silently think the word *Hum*. That's it. Set the timer for as long as you're going to meditate, and repeat this mantra over and over again until you're finished.

Another approach I teach my students who aren't comfortable using Sanskrit words is one I learned from my teacher, the late Dr. David Simon. As you follow your breath in, silently say *Just*. Then, as you follow your breath out, silently say *one*. Do this all the way until you reach the count of ten. Next, silently say the word *This*. As you follow your breath out, silently say *one*. Do this until you reach the count of ten. Finally, as you follow your breath in, silently say *Just*. Then, as you follow your breath out, silently say *This*. Repeat the mantra *Just This* for as long as you would like to continue your meditation.

A couple of things to note: You will have thoughts, you will become distracted by physical sensations in your body, and you will be pulled away from the repetition of the mantra by noises in the environment. This is normal and to be expected. Your intention is to simply notice when you've drifted away from the repetition of the mantra and choose to easily and effortlessly go back to it. There is no need to freak out that your meditation was disrupted, nor is there any reason for you to judge yourself or your experience. Everyone has thoughts at some point during meditation. We all forget to turn off our cell phone at least one time. No one is exempt from the fact that we live in a noisy, busy world. The key is to steal back time from the busyness of our days to connect inside—to find some stillness, some peace—so that we come from a place of being centered, grounded, and calm as we greet life.

Whether you sit for ten minutes or one hour a day, I guarantee that this will change your life for the better. All you need to do is find a quiet space, settle into a comfortable, seated position, close your eyes, and connect. I recommend you meditate a minimum of twenty minutes each day—first thing in the morning before you get started with your daily routine. Do it for twenty-one days in a row and notice how it becomes a powerful anchor.

Caring for Your Body: It's common knowledge that your physical health affects your mental and emotional health.

To maintain harmony physically, emotionally, mentally, and spiritually, it's important to have a daily routine of caring for your physical body—your foundation. Pay attention to your nutrition and hydration. Be sure to move your body every day and subscribe to some form of regular exercise. It's also imperative that you get restful sleep every night.

Everyone is different. You need to figure out what form of exercise benefits you, what best nourishes and fuels you in terms of nutrition, and the amount of sleep that is best for your own body. That being said, some basic guidelines and tips for nutrition are to avoid those middle aisles at the grocery store stocked with canned and boxed foods. Everything in those aisles is processed and can sit on a shelf for three to five years. Instead, do your best to shop the perimeter of the store, where you'll find fresh produce, fresh meats and dairy, and fresh-baked breads.

Another tip is to prep meals in advance. We're all so busy that it's a real temptation to eat fast food on the way home. Instead, prep your healthy meals in advance to take to work and keep at home. Fix several good meals and freeze them to pop in the oven when you get home. Minimize sugar, alcohol, and caffeine. Moderation is the key here. Do your best to make sure you're eating fresh, live, healthy foods that are as close to life force as possible.

In terms of movement and exercise, you've got hundreds of options. Choose something you enjoy so you'll stick with it and do it daily. Whether it's yoga classes, a gentle stretch on the living room floor, going for a run, taking a bike ride, or going for a brisk walk, focus on moving your body. Optimally, try to incorporate a practice of strength, balance, flexibility, and a little bit of cardio in your daily routine to keep your body healthy.

When it comes to sleep, there's a difference between getting enough sleep and getting *restful* sleep. Some people don't get enough sleep. If that's you, try to get yourself to bed at an earlier hour to get a full six to eight hours, whatever your body runs on optimally.

You might be getting enough sleep, yet still wake up feeling heavy and groggy. If this is the case, it may be that you're not getting restful sleep. Consider the current stressors in your daily life. What creates the mental agitation that wakes you up in the middle of the night? Avoid falling asleep with the television on, especially the news. Do some light reading before you go to bed, preferably reading something spiritual or lighthearted. Try lowering the lights earlier in the evening to support your circadian rhythm. Take a hot bath to ease into a nice, relaxed state just before bedtime.

Prioritize: How you spend your most precious resources—your time and energy—reveals what's important to you. Notice how you are—or aren't—putting time and energy into what you say you want. Does what you're doing support you in moving toward or away from what you say you want? What little things can you start doing each day to get you closer to who you want to be, closer to the things you are passionate and inspired about?

Being emotionally intelligent is an ongoing practice. Through the processes in this book, you may find that you're no longer looking in the rearview mirror and fumbling around in the past. When baggage shows up, you now know how to guide yourself through release processes. You now have tools to navigate your emotions in the moment. Your personal work does not end here. To step into the version of who it is you want to be and create a lifestyle you want to live, you have to stay committed to yourself and dedicate yourself to your practices daily.

If you know that skipping meditation means being less patient and more reactive, you need to be more committed to meditating than you are to whatever distracts you from meditating. If having a few cocktails before going to bed means you won't get a restful night of sleep, you need to be more committed to restful sleep than winding down with a drink.

The things you do each and every day are cumulative. You're not going to just do a practice once or twice and wake up to a magical new life for yourself. Just like going to the gym, you may not see results for a few weeks—yet you keep going to the gym because you know you're making progress. Likewise, our daily practices aren't instant fixes. The benefits show up the more we keep doing them.

Keep your focus forward. Look for the positive. Keep reframing. When you have a crummy day, it's okay to feel bad. That's part of being human. However, don't go using that one bad day to revisit old issues and stir up old stuff. Once you've done your release work, it serves no purpose whatsoever to go back and rehash it.

Of course, if you're doing a forgiveness process, you may need to spend some time recapitulating what happened in the past. There's purpose in that. But don't rehash the past and bring it into your present interactions and environment. Approach your present with a clean slate and your new foundation of emotional intelligence.

If you're anything like the old me, you're probably thinking, "Yeah right, I don't have the time to do any of these things during the day. That's just wishful thinking. I don't have so much as one spare moment to myself." If you're anything like the version of me when I began doing my personal development and healing work, you may have already started a huge list of all the new mindfulness-based lifestyle practices you're going to begin incorporating into your day starting tomorrow. Neither of these approaches are going to work in your favor. Two very important things you need to understand right here, right now: 1) You have to create the time for your daily practice, because the space in your schedule isn't necessarily going to open up all on its own, and 2) You have to start with baby steps, choosing one, *maybe* two things you'll do each day until those things become so ingrained in your daily routine that you don't even need to think about it anymore. That new practice is now just part of what you do every day. *Then* you add one, *maybe* two more things in.

We all have the same twenty-four hours in a day. It's what you choose to do with your time that will determine your quality of life. We always have a choice. Hit the snooze button a few more times or get up early and meditate. Spend time focusing on the negative or consciously choose to find the lesson in the experience. Hit happy hour after a long day at work or get some exercise. Wind down with an hour of television at night or take a hot shower and make some time to reflect on your day. Whatever you choose, choose wisely. Your choices are what create your reality, day after day.

9

Conscious Communication

"Promise you'll always remember: You're braver than you believe, and stronger than you seem, and smarter than you think."
- Christopher Robin to Pooh

Conscious communication is the art of effectively communicating with others in a way that increases the likelihood of having your needs met. It is expressing what needs to be said in a way that enables you to speak your truth without making the other person wrong. When delivered and received with the highest intention—with an open heart and open mind—conscious communication makes both parties feel heard. You both feel open and willing to resolve your conflict in a healthy, compassionate, and direct way.

We've all been on the giving and receiving end of harsh words and demanding tones. I think we can all agree this approach only makes things worse. The argument becomes more intense and breathes fire into the conflict. It creates more separation. Rather than bringing issues to a place of resolution, that contentious approach ends up making the situation worse. Slinging accusations about a person's character, their motives, or their behavior is completely counter-productive to finding positive resolution. Berating each other will escalate into a magnificent explosion, or one of you will pull back and disconnect.

This is the psychological equivalent of the fight-or-flight response: lashing out with our words or withdrawing from the conflict at hand and shutting down. Marriages have ended, friendships have dissolved, and family members have disowned each other because people don't know how to express their emotions and ask for what they need.

I've been guilty of this myself. In my youth, I had so much pent-up anger, resentment, and sadness that I blew up one day when I was fifteen. I moved out of my father's house, changed my last name to my mother's maiden name, and distanced myself from my family for the better part of twenty-five years. My relationship with my family blew up because I didn't know how to express my emotions or identify what I needed at the time. I didn't know how to engage in conscious communication as a means of resolving areas of conflict and confusion.

Four Questions for Conscious Communication

In my tenure at the Chopra Center for Well Being, I was introduced to the work of the late psychologist Dr. Marshall Rosenberg. I highly recommend his book *Nonviolent Communication* and its accompanying workbook (there is also one for teens that is absolutely fabulous!). I use his work as the basis of how I use and teach conscious communication today.

You prepare for conscious communication by asking some of the powerful questions we used in previous chapters, this time focused on communicating your needs. These questions set you up to craft and deliver your conscious communication.

Before doing so, however, remind yourself that people and situations that trigger you emotionally are sent to you as a gift. As human beings, we have the tendency to avoid discomfort by burying our emotions and sidestepping conflict. Despite that tendency, we are part of a universe that brings us exactly who and what we need in order to evolve and resolve anything that hinders that evolution.

Whenever something happens and you find yourself feeling emotionally charged, start by asking the four questions laid out below. I recommend you use your journal to record your thoughts and draft a conscious, direct, and thoughtful articulation of what you need to convey.

We've used similar questions to dig up baggage, to help you deal with emotions in the moment, and now for conscious communication. Here they are again:

1. "What happened?"

When we ask, "What happened?" many of us go off on a story full of judgment and accusation. Instead, become an observer. Do your best to simply observe the facts of what occurred. No story, no finger pointing, no assumptions, no melodrama— just what happened. Why?

Because when you launch into a story, three things happen. You create a story that is probably not even true. You make assumptions and judgments about a person with no real understanding of what's going on in their life. And you tend to make the story about you and take it personally. This stirs up the fight-or-flight response within us, which generates feelings of discomfort, gets us all wound up, and, by doing so, maybe gets everyone involved wound up as well. Whereas, if we just observe what happened, without any attachment, emotion, or melodrama, we stay in a calmer, more conscious state.

2. "What emotions am I feeling as a result of what happened?"

Take a deep breath and be present with the emotions you're feeling right now, in this moment. Identify those feelings. Are you feeling anger? Are you feeling resentment? Are you feeling fear or sadness? Next, take responsibility for what you feel, whatever the emotion is, and how you're interpreting what happened. How we interpret our experiences is what creates our reality. Own your emotion and interpretation. Your emotions and interpretations are not the other person's stuff; it's your stuff. It may have been generated as a result of something that happened, but it's still your stuff. Own it. Take responsibility and abstain from thinking this person or that situation is responsible for making you feel whatever you feel. Avoid any victimizing language.

3. "What do I need that I'm not getting in this situation?"

This is tricky for many people. We tend to expect others to know what our needs are and to meet them without being given any direction—even if we don't even know ourselves what we need in a given scenario. An interesting phenomenon that we all do, to some extent, is expect other people to know what we need. We expect them to then meet that need for us. Isn't that interesting? We expect that our parents or our spouse or our friends should be able to guess at or intuit what we need, and for them to then immediately find a way to make us feel safe, comforted, and appreciated. What's even crazier to think about is that ninety percent of the time, *we* don't even know what we need in the moment—at least, not consciously—and yet we expect those closest to us to look into a crystal ball and figure it out on our behalf. It's kind of absurd when you think about it, isn't it? This is an important step in this part of the self-inquiry, as it puts us in the position of taking responsibility for knowing what we need so we can then go about discerning how to get our needs met in more realistic and healthy ways.

As children, we don't identify what we need because our parents provide everything for us. As babies, and young children, and even young adults, we simply rely on our parents to meet all our needs for food, shelter, love, and guidance—and whatever else we need. Once we enter the real world, we get pissed off or hurt when people around us fall short in anticipating our needs.

Get clear on what you needed during whatever happened. When you become clear about what you need, you will be clear and concise in what you're asking for as you're communicating with others.

4. "What am I asking for the other person to do, or how do I want the other person to show up?"

This can be scary. You can't be certain about how the other person will respond. Before identifying what you are going to ask the other person for, you must be willing to enter a space of vulnerability and know that the outcome is totally unpredictable. This can be one of the greatest challenges for people when actually delivering the communication calmly and consciously.

Knowing this upfront, carefully consider what you will ask of the other person. You must be specific. Ambiguities will not get you the results that you're hoping for, and neither will demands.

When you deliver your communication, *ask* for what you need in the form of a request as opposed to an ultimatum or demand. No one responds well to threats. Take into consideration how you would feel if someone addressed you as you intend to address the other person. Set yourself up for success by helping them *understand* you rather than push back against you.

Conscious Versus Unconscious Communication

Let's run through some examples of how conscious communication might work in different situations:

Say that every Thursday morning at 9 a.m., your company has a team meeting, and one of your coworkers shows up twenty to twenty-five minutes late each week. The meeting doesn't get started until he arrives.

What just happened? This man has been twenty-five minutes late to the meeting every week for three weeks. Period. Don't create a story about how inconsiderate and disrespectful that person is. Don't add, "How can he get away with that behavior in the workplace? Why isn't he being called out or fired?" Just look at the facts of what happened, which is that your co-worker has been late by twenty-five minutes every Thursday for the past three weeks in a row. Period.

What emotions are you feeling about that? In this case, you might feel angry or frustrated. Acknowledge those feelings and own them as yours. Refrain from using words like "disrespected" or "patronized." Those are words of victimization. Avoid pointing the finger and thinking that he "made" you feel a certain way. He didn't. You're experiencing those emotions based on your interpretation of what was happening.

What did you need that you weren't getting? Maybe your need at the time was to feel respected or like your time was as valuable as his. Maybe you just needed to know that he was going to be late so you could get other work done rather than putting your deadlines on hold while waiting in the conference room.

What specifically are you asking the other person to do? You might ask him to show up on time or call if he is going to be late. Those are clearly defined actions that he can choose to take or not. But asking for something like, "I need you to respect me and my time" or "I need you to be responsible" are too vague. His definition of respect or what it means to be responsible might be quite different than yours. And his being late may have nothing to do with respect or responsibility in his mind.

Let's try another example, this time of a married couple. The husband has worked late for three months straight, sometimes coming home as late as 11 p.m., Monday through Friday. His wife is becoming increasingly agitated. She's at home, raising the kids, working full time, and feeling overloaded with picking up the kids from school, grocery shopping, laundry, homework, and soccer practice. Because she's not expressing this to him, her anger and upset is slowly building. She's creating a story in her mind that maybe he's not even at work. Maybe he's having an affair. Or, maybe his work is more important and he just doesn't care about her and the family.

Because we aren't taught how to communicate well, what often happens in this situation? One night, he comes home late and she absolutely flies off the handle. She goes into a rant: "Oh, how nice of you *finally* make it home! Why are you staying out so late? Are you even at the office? You're never here, you don't care about me, you don't care about your kids. Why are we even in this marriage?" Her husband has just come through the door and is blasted with her anger and overwhelm. How do you think he's going to respond? He'll likely either lash out at her, or throw his hands up in the air, walk right past her, take a shower, and go straight to bed. Nothing is resolved, and she's left to just fester in her upset.

This is unfortunately what happens in a lot of marriage communication. We bury our stuff until we pop, resulting in an explosive outburst. Things are said and things are done that can't be taken back. Then, we bury it again until the next time we blow up. Using the four questions, what could she have done instead?

What just happened? "My husband has been getting home as late as 11 p.m. for three months. I have been handling all of our household and child-raising responsibilities."

What feelings are generated? "I feel hurt, angry, and a little frightened. I also feel exhausted and overwhelmed."

What needs weren't being met? "I need to feel loved and supported. I need help with the household and children. I need to feel intimately connected with my husband."

What specifically am I asking for? "I want him to spend time with me and the children in the evenings. I want him to help with some of the chores and responsibilities of our family. I want the two of us to spend more time together as a couple on weekends, maybe have a date night once a week."

If this woman takes the time to move through the four questions, here's how the interaction might go: When her husband comes through the door, she greets him with, "Hi, honey, it's late. You must be exhausted. Let me take your jacket. I have some things I'd like to share with you that have been on my mind. Is now a good time?" Notice that she set herself up for a better interaction by checking that this was a good time for him. If he's exhausted, it's probably not the best time to talk. Give the other person an opportunity to say, "Yes, this is a great time," or "No, I need to get some sleep. Can we come back to it in the morning?"

If the time is right, she might say, "Hey, honey, I've noticed that for the past three months you've been coming home at 11 p.m., Monday through Friday." That's what happened. Period. No melodrama. "I'm starting to feel a little frustrated and I'm noticing that I'm also feeling some resentment starting to build up. I want to have this conversation with you to share what I'm feeling."

Next, she'd express her needs: "I did some thinking about it to get clear on what I need. It occurred to me that what I need is to spend more quality time with you. I need to feel connected with you and like we're on the same page. I need to have a date night with you. I need to make love, I need to laugh more, I need to re-establish our connection because I miss you and I miss us."

Finally, she would ask him to do something to fill her needs: "So, what do you say that on Friday nights, we go on a date night? Can you let your office know that you need to leave by 5, or can you be home by 6 p.m. so that we can have dinner together as a family with the kids? After they're in bed, we could put on a great movie and just hang out on the couch, or make love, or just talk? Or maybe we could hire a babysitter and go out on a dinner date, then go see a movie? Would that be something you'd be willing to do each week?"

Her husband can then choose. He might say, "Oh my gosh, sweetheart, I had no idea that it was having this effect on you. I'm so sorry. Yes, of course, our relationship is so important to me. I've been missing you too, and the kids as well. Yes. Friday nights I will be home before 6 p.m.—we'll have dinner together and then have some romantic time just the two of us." They've come to a resolution. This is the best possible outcome.

Or, he might just say, "I can't do it. I'm a new attorney in this law firm and if I want to make partner, I've got to put in a lot of hours." He's not being a jerk. It's just that he's in a bind. He's got these responsibilities at work, so he's not able to meet her needs at this time. They then have the opportunity to figure out a compromise that allows him to put in the hours he needs while finding time to be together as a couple and family.

Of course, there is also the chance that her husband might not be interested in meeting her needs at all. "You're so needy. Get off my back. If you weren't swiping my credit card all day, I wouldn't have to work until midnight. You're paranoid if you think I'm out sleeping with somebody else." If this is the case, she then has the opportunity to choose whether to stay in the relationship or consider leaving the relationship so that she is able to meet her needs elsewhere. It's a harsh reality and, let's face it, doing any kind of personal development work means being willing to face the truth and make difficult decisions.

This example brings up an important point: What if the other person won't do what you want them to do? What if they get angry in response to your request? What if they can't do it, or refuse to do it? Our intention is to open a line of communication that serves both sides. Yet sometimes, the other person isn't willing or able to meet your needs. Perhaps your needs are in direct conflict with their own, and meeting your needs would mean not honoring their own. Or the other person may simply not care to meet your needs. In that case, they may respond with a snide comment or some nasty remark, and blow you off completely.

In both instances, the only thing you can do is accept what is. Take responsibility for how you feel and respond in a way that moves you toward finding a solution. It's impossible to change another person. As we all very well know, it's hard enough to change ourselves. We don't have control over anything except our own thoughts, words, and actions. We have no control over what other people do, or how life unfolds. We do, however, have a choice in how we will choose to respond.

Save yourself a tremendous amount of time and energy by not trying to convince the other person to see your point of view and change their position. Redirect that time and energy into taking a closer look at this relationship. Do you want to continue investing your precious time and energy into it? Can you honor where the other person is coming from and do your best to find compromise where both of you feel safe in expressing yourselves, even though you don't share the same opinion or the same desires? We're not just talking about intimate relationships here. We're also talking about friendships, inter-office relationships, and even relationships with family members.

When someone cannot or will not meet your needs, use the steps for navigating your emotions in the moment: lean into the emotions you feel, release anything that does not serve you, and consciously choose how you want to move forward.

If you practice using conscious communication with the small issues, you'll be much more adept at using this skill when the big ones hit. Even small irritations can build up. She leaves her shoes all over the house. He calls her too often while she's at the office. That coworker "borrows" other people's food from the breakroom refrigerator. Use conscious communication for any of these small irritants. It will not only sharpen your skills, but it will keep tiny issues from becoming massive ordeals. In some cases, you may also need to enforce boundaries.

The Importance of Boundaries

In navigating our emotions every day, it's imperative that we learn to set and maintain boundaries in every area of our lives, both with ourselves and with others. A boundary is an invisible line we draw in the sand. Determining a boundary declares what is most important to us, and lets people know our parameters for what is acceptable and what is not.

Identifying a boundary is really asking yourself, "What am I willing to do or not do? What am I willing to accept or not accept in terms of how someone else is treating me?"

Boundaries, like emotions, are based on our needs: our need for safety, inclusion, or respect. In many cases, when a person doesn't know how to get their needs met, they compromise their boundaries and become people pleasers.

For example, someone might overwork and not honor their own need for downtime and rest in an attempt to get validation from their coworkers or boss. We call this a self-inflicted boundary violation. You know you need downtime and rest, yet you ignore that need and work harder to feel validated. You've run over your own boundary.

Another example is going with the flow in social settings so people will like you. You say "yes" to a social engagement even though you'd really prefer to do something else. Disregarding your own preferences, you put your party shoes on and head out to prove that you can be one of the gang. Ultimately, this boundary violation leads to resentment toward yourself and others. Resentment is a key indicator that your boundary has been violated.

If we don't set and maintain boundaries with ourselves, it's especially difficult to set and maintain boundaries with anybody else. A boundary you set with someone else might sound like: "I need you to not call me after 9:30 p.m. so I can get the rest I need." "I need you to give me lead time when project priorities change so I can rearrange my workload." "Shouting or storming around the house when you've had a bad day is not working for me. I need you to take a deep breath before you come in the front door and be kind to the children and me." "I need you to speak softly until I've had my first cup of coffee in the morning." That's a definite boundary for me in the mornings! A boundary can also be about feeling safe: "I need you to refrain from becoming physically or verbally abusive when we have an argument." "I need you to call me and let me know that you're okay when you're out late."

Similar to violating your own boundaries, you feel resentment when someone else runs over your boundaries. You become angry, or feel overwhelmed and depleted. You're letting what other people *want* become more important than what you *need*. If you aren't used to setting boundaries, you may not even know consciously what your boundaries are. Pay attention when emotions like resentment, anger, sadness, or overwhelm pop up. If you trace back to the incident that elicited that feeling, you'll probably find a boundary violation.

Setting boundaries is important in all areas of our lives. You may be good at setting boundaries in one area but not another. For example, I see many high-powered women who know exactly where their boundaries are at work, but when they get into romantic relationships, they let their partners walk all over them.

I see a lot of parents who are good boundary-setters in relationships or careers, but when it comes to their kids, they give in and let their kids have full reign. When parents are strong in setting and upholding their boundaries, their children will learn to operate within the parameters provided. But if parents give in as soon as children act out, the children know that they have no boundaries and can get whatever they want by throwing a tantrum. This isn't healthy for children when they're young, but is even worse as they become adults heading out into the world. Setting boundaries with your kids teaches them the importance of respecting other people's boundaries as well as enforcing their own.

Here's the bottom line: If you don't set and maintain boundaries with other people, they will continue to run over them. When your boundaries are violated, what happens? You start to feel frustrated or sad, resentful or angry. Over time, this can have a detrimental effect on your self-worth, your self-esteem. When someone runs over your boundary, it's up to you to let them know it's not okay.

On another note, you can't expect someone to honor your boundary if you haven't even told them what it is. Our friends, family, and coworkers are not mind-readers. Once you recognize that you have a boundary, you're responsible for making it clear to others. Set the boundary clearly using conscious communication. You set the boundary saying, "Here's what I need in a relationship. Are you able to meet me here in this space?" If the person says no, you're in a different conversation. The question becomes, "Do I need to be in this relationship?" You've stated your boundaries, maybe they've stated theirs. If there isn't a coherence or a way to compromise that works for both of you, then you don't have a solid relationship. Whatever the context of the relationship is, honoring boundaries keeps it on an even playing ground. Both parties come together and honor and respect one another, with a clear understanding of the conditions of the situation.

Let's look at boundaries in different areas of your life. In the area of health and fitness, a healthy boundary with your partner might be that you value health and wellness. You want to eat a certain way and work out every day. Your partner doesn't need to have the same values, just to honor yours. A very healthy boundary with your partner or friends might be, "Hey, working out every day is important to me for my overall health and well-being. I'd like to ask for your support in making sure I get out the door to the gym every day. So instead of saying to me, 'Please don't go to the gym today. I really wanted to hang out with you,' help me by encouraging me to get my workout in."

Boundaries in the workplace can be tricky. For example, I know a woman (we'll call her Carrie) who worked for a great company, but she found herself, along with all her coworkers, working sixty to seventy hours per week. Carrie's weekends were eaten up with the company's special events, and she often got less than five to six hours per week of downtime to herself. After three or four years of this, she was overwhelmed, fatigued, stressed out, and near adrenal burn out. She wasn't sleeping well or eating healthy meals, and she knew something had to give.

Carrie decided she was going to start working the hours that were laid out in her job description rather than the crazy hours she'd been working up to that point. She wasn't going to slack off or cop a bad attitude. Carrie was determined to give a hundred percent at her job—but not two hundred percent. She got to work at 8 a.m. and left at 5 p.m., even going out during her lunch break rather than eating at her desk.

Within a short time, Carrie began to get a lot of pushback from her manager and her coworkers. But she stayed firm with her boundary. When she was questioned about leaving at 5 p.m. while others were still working, she replied, "I'm not leaving early. I'm leaving on time. And I need to take care of myself so I can be at my best on this job and balanced in the rest of my life." Eventually, when her manager saw the quality of work Carrie could produce and her coworkers saw how much healthier and happier she was, things started to change in her department. Coworkers started setting healthier work hours for themselves and managers became more supportive.

As Carrie said years later, "It was a healthy boundary for three reasons. Number one, it enabled me to get out of the office and start taking care of myself. And number two, it let the people around me know that I wasn't going to be taken for granted, that I wasn't just a work horse. They began to respect me. It challenged me to go outside of my comfort zone and become stronger. Last, I even noticed that my actions of enforcing this boundary became a healthy example for others."

That's what setting and maintaining boundaries does for you. It empowers you. It lets other people know what's acceptable and what's not acceptable. It inspires everyone who's observing you to think, "Hey, if she can do that, I can do that, too." It inspires them to start setting and maintaining stronger boundaries in their own lives. It's especially important for children to observe this type of behavior.

Let's contrast with another true story. A woman (we'll call her Jennifer) worked on an elite sales team that went after national accounts for her company. This meant that Jennifer not only traveled across the country every week, but she put in at least seventy hours per week, working at night, at home, or in her hotel room. She didn't feel that she could give up this job even though she knew it was unhealthy for her. Where else would she find the income and prestige it gave her? So, she hung in there and her bosses continued to pile more accounts on her plate. After six months of this, Jennifer's decision was made for her: Her back went out and she was totally bedridden for three weeks. Her division went through restructuring and, while she was still laid up, she was laid off.

The story has a positive ending in that Jennifer found a new career that made her much happier. But if she had recognized the symptoms of burnout and had been willing to set clear, healthy boundaries, she wouldn't have experienced the trauma of her body giving out on her.

One of my own experiences where a boundary needed to be set is not uncommon. I was living with a guy who was often on the road for work. Things were not great between us. I heard from a friend of mine (unbeknownst to my boyfriend) who happened to be on the road with my boyfriend. He was calling to tell me that my boyfriend was seeing another woman.

When my boyfriend came back, I had the opportunity to go through his text messages, and basically saw everything I needed to see to know it was true. When I asked him about it, he told me it was none of my business what he did on the road. We were living together, and I'd moved all the way across the country with him. At that point, I had to decide, "What will I tolerate in intimate relationships? Where is the line that I draw in the sand? Am I going to stay in this relationship with someone who clearly has no accountability, no sense of responsibility, and certainly no respect for me or our relationship?"

First, I gave him the option: "This doesn't work for me. This lying, this going behind my back, it doesn't work for me. Are you in a space where you want to make this relationship work? Yes or no?" His answer was no. I had to uphold a boundary with myself and him: "Okay, this relationship is done. I need to go."

Many people I coach have family members or intimate partners who run over their boundaries. For example, one of my clients has a son who acts like a spoiled brat. He torments his father, telling him what a disappointment he is, and that he only tolerates him because he has to. In the next breath, the son will insist that his father send him rent money. My client has already put his son through three Ivy League colleges and pays all his bills. Yet, he's never demanded that his son treat him with respect or face the consequences of getting a job and paying for his own education.

When it comes to dealing with other people, a boundary isn't really a boundary until you've identified it, communicated it, and followed through on it. You might assume that anyone with a lick of common sense would know that you can't be horrible to someone and expect them to continue supporting you. Apparently, this son didn't know that and had never been told that. My client needed to be clear and say, "This is a boundary for me. You can no longer treat me this way. You can't call me up and be nasty to me. If you continue to do so, be very clear that I will not pay your rent or support you financially in any way." Then my client needed to be willing to follow through with his word, cutting his son off if he violated the boundary again.

A boundary is only a real boundary when you've set it. You can't hold someone accountable for violating that boundary unless they know it's there.

Setting boundaries can be tough. What if you're in a relationship and your need is to experience multiple partners? You're afraid of hurting your partner, but you want to be responsible. Instead of cheating on your current relationship, you can honor both of you by having an honest conversation about wanting an open relationship. This allows your partner the option of being okay with that arrangement or leaving the relationship. We all have needs that we need to have met to stay true to ourselves. We all have boundaries we need to set to stay true to our path and our purpose.

In a conversation around setting a boundary, be upfront about where you stand, what your position is, and what your needs are. Bring the conversation to the table instead of running a hidden agenda behind the scenes.

Just by the sheer nature of boundaries, somebody is going to bump up against them and experience hurt. Your parents might want you to come for the holidays and you might say, "Mom and Dad, I'm going to stay here and spend the holidays with my new fiancé, just the two of us." It might create some upset. In this instance, you simply apologize that you've disappointed them and move on. It might be uncomfortable, but it's much better than violating your own boundaries with the resulting anger and resentment.

Like using conscious communication, setting and enforcing boundaries takes time and practice. It's simple, and yet, it's not always easy. Can you remember learning how to ride a bicycle and how frightening it was? Day after day, you practiced one thing, then the next. Within a few weeks, you rode off without your training wheels and your foundation was established. Every day, you learned something new. Sometimes you wiped out, and other times you rode seamlessly without a hitch. Every day was something new. And so is the journey of personal development.

This is Not the End, It's Just the Beginning

"You stand at the threshold of a grand adventure. And the extent to which you are able to experience the fullness of that journey is determined by the extent to which you are able to let go of the scenarios that no longer serve you."

\- Rasha in *Oneness*

The art of becoming an emotionally empowered human being is a skillset you must mindfully practice with diligence, patience, and awareness. You must hold the intention to unfold potential and maintain your willingness to do whatever it takes to evolve into a person you can truly love and respect.

Today, my father and I have a loving friendship, deep spiritual connection, and level of understanding with one another. We were very blessed to have this happy ending. My mother and I have learned to respect each other's boundaries; she's my best friend, and we cherish the time we get to spend with one another.

I went through a gradual process of dropping my armor and lowering the walls I had built around me. I moved into a more open, expanded, and compassionate heart-space as a result of meditation, doing emotional release work, and taking the time to understand myself and my parents. I also learned about conscious communication and how to resolve our differences through the art of listening and speaking my truth with kindness, compassion, and an open heart. I forgave my parents and myself, because we were all doing the best we knew how at the time, and we're different people now.

In the pages of this book, I've guided you on the path I took to heal myself, to heal my relationships with the people I love, and to ultimately step into the woman I am today. It's my hope that this book encourages you to find the clarity, compassion, strength, and fortitude within yourself to go the distance on your own path—and to truly heal your heart.

"The breezes at dawn have secrets to tell you
Don't go back to sleep!
You must ask for what you really want.
Don't go back to sleep!
People are going back and forth across the
doorsill where the two worlds touch,
The door is round and open
Don't go back to sleep!"

- Rumi

About the Author

Tris Thorp is one of today's leading experts in the field of emotional healing. Having spent the last decade traveling the world, trained by and sharing the stage with Dr. Deepak Chopra in the field of consciousness and mindfulness-based practices, Tris has a real gift for integrating ancient spiritual teachings with modern-day mindfulness to help people all over the world let go of their past and create an empowered new future.

During her tenure at the Chopra Center, Tris apprenticed under the Chopra Center's co-founder Dr. David Simon, co-facilitating the Healing the Heart and Emotional Freedom workshops alongside him. Prior to his untimely passing, Dr. Simon appointed Tris as the person to carry on his teachings in the field of emotional healing.

In addition, Tris was fortunate to be mentored by the late Debbie Ford prior to her passing, where she continued her extensive studies of the unconscious mind and concepts of the persona and shadow. After the loss of her two beloved teachers and mentors, Tris went on to become certified through the Ford Institute as a coach specializing in shadow work and reconciling mental and emotional issues stemming from past experiences. She continues to share the gifts of emotional healing and facilitates this work in the footsteps of her former mentors.

Tris is the co-author of Mental and Emotional Release® with Dr. Matt James. Written in a language both professionals and non-professionals can understand, Mental and Emotional Release® offers real life case studies, an overview of MER and its foundation, step-by-step scripts to follow, and clinical efficacy studies comparing MER to other therapies.

Clearly in her dharma, Tris' passion and dedication to gently guide people on their inward journey through emotional healing is evident in her work as a Lead Trainer/Facilitator with The Empowerment Partnership. She teaches various classes on ego, persona and shadow personal empowerment, emotional healing, and higher states of consciousness at iNLP Master Practitioner Training, the Empowering Your Life weekend, and at the Huna—ancient energy healing and spiritual shamanism of ancient Hawaii—on the Big Island of Hawaii.

Tris Thorp is Board Certified by the Association of Integrative Psychology as a Trainer of NLP, Master Practitioner of Neuro Linguistic Programming, Hypnosis, and Mental and Emotional Release®, a certified Reiki Master, certified Breakthrough Shadow Coach through The Ford Institute and a certified Integrative NLP Coach through the Association for Integrative Psychology. Tris is an Experienced Yoga Teacher with Yoga Alliance. She is certified by Dr. Deepak Chopra in Primordial Sound Meditation, Perfect Health: Ayurvedic Lifestyle, and Seven Spiritual Laws of Yoga.

Tris is devoted to inspiring and empowering others to cultivate and maintain mindfulness-based lifestyle practices that lead to greater clarity, purpose and fulfillment. Through one-on-one coaching, online programs, and live events, Tris specializes in helping people to fully release negative emotions, limiting beliefs, and unconscious patterns, enabling them to make quantum leaps into the life they are truly meant to be living.

You can learn more about Tris and her work as a public speaker, author, facilitator, and lifestyle and leadership coach at www.tristhorp.com, and on Facebook at https://www.facebook.com/TrisThorpLifestyleDesign/.

Connect with the Author

Website: www.tristhorp.com

Email: tris@tristhorp.com

Social Media:

Facebook: https://www.facebook.com/
TrisThorpLifestyleDesign/

Instagram: https://www.instagram.com/tristhorp/

Other books by Tris:

Mental and Emotional Release® by Dr. Matt James with Tris Thorp – Balboa Publishing 2017

https://amzn.to/2GyKCbS

Acknowledgements

Who I've become wouldn't have been possible without four incredible people. The late Dr. David Simon, davidji, the late Debbie Ford, and Deepak Chopra have all contributed in their own way to shape the person I am today. Each are a solid pillar for the foundation I now stand upon, and I am forever humbled for having been graced by their mentorship. To have learned from one of them in a single lifetime would have been an incredible honor. To have one of them in each of my corners simultaneously created an energetic vortex of spiritual connection, healing, transformation, vision, and empowerment.

David Simon

You played so many roles in my life—from mentor to teacher, from friend to confidante. Your presence provided me with the opportunity to heal my wounds and create an unimaginable new life for myself. You taught me that experience and knowledge go hand in hand, and when both come together wisdom is born. You saw something in me all those years ago that I wasn't able to see myself, and you set me on my path to helping others heal their past. Who you are to me can never be expressed in words, and I am forever grateful to have learned from you, shared the stage with you, and accepted the torch you passed when you left this world. I know I make you proud.

davidji

You have been my inspiration for a decade. Your sheer brilliance, your courage, and your fortitude to live in your highest dharma are unparalleled. Your camaraderie, love, and support have been a candle in the window more times than I can count. We have shared laughter; we have shared tears. We've celebrated our greatest wins and our deepest losses. You have shown me what it means to walk the path with truth, integrity, and grace while keeping it real. You are the teachings.

Debbie Ford
I'll never forget when David first sent me to work with you. I thought you were the most beautiful, powerful, and intimidating woman I'd ever met. As I came to know you and your heart, I saw myself in you, and that terrified me. You showed me that my biggest flaws were my greatest assets, and then you taught me how to wield them for the purpose of healing my heart. The last time I saw you, we hugged. As we pulled away, you looked in my eyes and said, "You're ready now." I don't think I believed you. And then you left this world a short time later and I knew that with both you and David gone, I had to be ready. Thank you, Debbie, for your heart, your work, and for believing in me. I love you dearly.

Deepak Chopra
The world knows you as the most influential and important pioneer of consciousness and neuroscience of all time. Humanity is better because of you and the teachings you share so tirelessly. I have been blessed with the opportunity to witness your heart and learn from you firsthand. The decade I got to spend working with you was full of growth, expansion, and most importantly love. Thank you for all your guidance, support, and friendship over the years. I am forever grateful.

References

www.empowermentpartnership.com

www.nlp.com

www.tristhorp.com

Resources

Brown, Michael, *The Presence Process*

Davidji, *Secrets of Meditation*

James, Dr. Matt, *Find Your Purpose: Master Your Path*

James, Dr. Matt, *Ho'oponopono*

James, Dr. Matt, *Integrate the Shadow: Master Your Path*

James, Dr. Matt, Thorp, Tris, *Mental and Emotional Release*

Rosenberg, Marshall, *Nonviolent Communication*

Walsch, Neale Donald, *The Little Soul and the Sun*

Made in the USA
San Bernardino, CA
16 May 2018